DEAR FELLOW

Dreamer

Waking Up,
Taking Chances,
and Creating
a Life of
Your Own

EMILY BURNETT

Paperback ISBN 979-8-9886775-1-2 Ellis Lane Press First Edition, November 2025.

To the ones who've believed in me: I'm deeply grateful. And to every dreamer who reads this: I believe in you.

DISCLAIMER

A Note on Names

I've changed the names of people who appear in this book—not because their identities need protecting or because I've written anything I consider unflattering, but because these are my experiences and my reflections. What I've learned and appreciated about others may not align perfectly with how they see themselves or our shared moments, and that's okay. There is no way to write about my life and lessons without referencing other people (not that I'd even want to), but since the stories are written from my perspective and through my lens, it made sense to change names.

On Advice (or Lack Thereof)

Nothing in this book should be construed as professional advice tailored to your specific situation. I'm sharing reflections, stories, and what I've learned—not prescribing what you should do. Your cool life, your cool decisions.

CONTENTS

To live is the rarest thing in the world, most people only exist.

Oscar Wilde

PREFACE

When I first started writing this book, which I knew pretty quickly would be named *Dear Fellow Dreamer*, I found myself grossly oversimplifying the process of dreaming big. This, even though my own experiences were teaching me that nothing as worthwhile as pursuing a dream is as neat and tidy as a step-by-step list.

1. You have a dream.

2. You prepare to leap toward it.

3. You leap.

4. You go through a little uncertainty.

5. You get your dream. Yay!

After writing the first draft of this book, I realized I couldn't—and didn't want to—force something as wonderfully untamable as big dreams into a formulaic box. And I shelved it for several months to grapple with what I've learned about having dreams, waking up, taking chances, and the relationship between dreams and contentment.

The book you've just picked up is infinitely better for the pause, for the further excavation of thought I put into it. For the tears, the endless re-writing, thinking of what I wanted to share with fellow dreamers, and asking myself hard questions. The version you're holding in your hands now does a much better job of honoring the uniqueness of each of our dreams and our roads toward them. It includes more of my faith in God, who I believe made us to dream and seek and explore and walk by faith down here.

Even after these critical refinements, however, I found myself hesitating to get this book over the finish line. Why? Well, a book like this never actually feels finished. I also know my thoughts on the matter will continue to evolve and mature. Playing a bigger role, though, was that *I* was waiting to see how my dreams worked out—a neat and tidy finale would be *just* the successful bow to put on the whole package.

But what does "worked out" even mean? Especially when I've learned that our dreams are starting lines and North Stars more than they are finish lines? I've finally decided to take some of my own advice and share this with you right now, right where I am. It could be that the *whole point* of it is that it is written from me in the middle to you in whatever your beginning or middle looks like. So here goes nothing, or here goes something pretty cool for all of us.

Emily

INTRODUCTION

"Do any of you actually *care* about this?" Throughout my corporate years, I'd find myself looking around in especially stale meetings in excessively air-conditioned office buildings, studying the faces of my fellow meeting attendees.

I wasn't sure they did. I wasn't sure I did.

Of course, I cared about showing up and doing a great job. I liked my work and my work people. Some days I even loved both. The commute usually wasn't bad. The salary and benefits were great. Some projects were particularly satisfying and we often had fun solving problems together and socializing as coworkers are wont to do.

But I perpetually found myself more interested in the potential of each person in the company, from the newest entry-level employee to CEO. We're not talking about their HR-sanctioned, corporate-approved potential. Oh no. What interested me was their intrinsic, soul-level potential. I wanted to know what their kid selves would think of their adult lives. Were they actually as "obsessed" as the company wanted them to be and they claimed to be with the company's mission or their particular role? How much were they directing their own lives versus trying to outearn and outspend a life they didn't really like? What were their buried hopes and dreams for life, for family, for creating something of their own?

Sadly, no one was paying me to be a dreamer or a life coach, so I mostly reconciled myself to doing my job well, tried repeatedly to reinvest in whichever company employed me at the time, practice more gratitude and presence, and be content with dabbling in my own side hustles. It would work for a time, but the thing about dreams and "the call of the wild" is that they can be awfully persistent.

Fast forward several years. We weren't supposed to be awake for our arrival in the New York Harbor on December 19. But a ginormous storm threatened our final stop in Bermuda, so we skipped it and made directly for New York City instead, arriving thirty-six hours ahead of schedule. The couple who planned to marry in an exotic island wedding were wed instead on the boat by the captain once we entered U.S. waters. The groom's spirits didn't seem to be remotely dampened; he celebrated his nuptials by walking around the deck in a blazer and his underwear, freezing temperatures be danged.

How'd I get here? Somewhere in the middle of a midlife exploration session, I found myself on a boat—a big one—heading from Rome to New York. These boats are typically called ships, and the whole experience is typically called a cruise; I just found it infinitely more fun and appropriate to call the whole experience a "boat journey." Especially given that the boat was my ride back to the U.S. from Europe and a cheap place to live for more than two weeks.

As we sailed down the Hudson in grand style at mid-day, we oohed and aahed over all the iconic sights we would've slept through had things gone according to plan. Passengers and crew alike crowded the decks to marvel over the likes of Lady Liberty, the Brooklyn Bridge, Ellis Island, and a landscape of skyscrapers. All these were posed against a backdrop of the darkest storm clouds you've ever seen; if we'd had a supersized villain and a humble superhero, we would have had a scene straight out of a Marvel movie.

Meeting two of my Canadian boat buddies on the deck, we got to chatting with a young, honeymooning couple from Argentina. The canvas shoes I'd picked up in Lisbon as the only other closed-toe alternative I had to boots were nowhere near warm enough to keep my feet warm. I really could've used a scarf since it was legitimately freezing, but I didn't want to duck down to my cabin for it and lose my prime spot at the railing. Or miss any part of what was going on. And while I'm talking about not wanting to miss any part of an actual experience, I'm also talking metaphorically about not wanting to miss out on *life*.

The previous year, I felt God beckoning me out of an impressive comfort zone to go explore—new parts of the world, loads of new people, my business and life goals, my thoughts on entrepreneurship, how we all measure success, what it looks like to live by faith. Once I finally worked up my courage to listen, I put my house on the market, put in three weeks' notice at work, and bought a one-way ticket to Rome for the start of the new year. Why Rome? Because *why not* Rome? Everyone who can ought to see Rome in their lifetime.

And you would not *believe* just how quickly and miraculously everything worked out—I met the love of my life while traveling, all my business goals were met and wildly exceeded, and I am writing to you from my ranch in Montana.

But actually, it hasn't quite worked out like all that. Gotcha!

Maybe you were cheering for me, saying, "That's so cool!" Or maybe you were rolling your eyes at my easy success. Don't get me wrong, the above is certainly the way I hoped it all would work out. There's just something so validating when things fall into place immediately after bold action. If you succeed wildly according to the definitions and timelines of others, people clap and cheer and say, "You were right!" They throw parties. You throw parties. Your leap of faith receives a universal stamp of approval.

But when you get a more, ah, interesting road of discovery and exploration, there can be less clapping and cheering and more low-grade confusion. Which just means digging deep into what it really means to have dreams, to believe in God, to believe in yourself, and to take action in the direction of those dreams.

This book is not a heavily researched, science-backed "here's what the experts say or here's what the evidence tells us" experience. Oh heck naw. Nothing wrong with experts or evidence. It's just that *you* get to be the expert on your own dreams and run your own experiments to get your own evidence.

This is not a book that promises to solve your problems. Only you and God have those answers. It's not even a traditional chapter book. And it's not a book about Santa—sorry to a disappointed six-year-old girl named Zoe in North Carolina who was really hoping this would be that. This book is from someone super human. Not superhuman, but super *human* if you know what I mean.

It's meant to be the sort of book you can pop in and out of and take with you (figuratively or literally) on your own journey of exploration and risk-taking. Because this whole living-a-meaningful-life business is highly personalized and non-linear, *Dear Fellow Dreamer* is organized in sections according to what you might need:

- **Wake-up Calls**: Reminders that your life and your dreams matter. A lot.

- **Permission Slips**: For the days when you find yourself discounting or doubting your right to have dreams or keep dreaming.

- **Frequently Asked Questions**: We may not say them out loud, but these questions can get awfully noisy rattling around in our brains.

- **Trail Markers**: Practical reminders and lessons I've learned from exploring, and advice I still use.

- **Field Notes**: My own lessons and pinch-me moments from "the field" otherwise known as years of risking and trying and "failing" and doing my darndest to really live.

This collection of essays, vignettes, stories, recommendations, and questions is written by your friend on the same quest to live meaningfully, and who wants to see you succeed and risk and get lots of scuffs and battle scars and experience more moments of stretching and exhilaration than you can currently imagine.

Speaking of imagination, in a life where you're trying to create something of your own, you will have more pinch-me moments than you can currently imagine. More tears, too. But the alternative is some version of a numb life and I suspect we'll both take the tears over that, for the sake of really living, not just existing.

BONUS: Be sure to visit emilyburnett.me/dreamer to get the PDF resources I created to accompany this book. They're designed to get you talking with yourself about your dreams, working up your courage, and celebrating just how far you've already come.

1

WAKE-UP CALLS

Mel Robbins wrote a gangbusters book called *The 5 Second Rule.* This "rule" came about in a time in her life when she needed to prompt herself to necessary action with a simple process of counting backward from five. At risk of stating the obvious, the process goes a little something like this: "Five...four...three...two...one." When you reach one, you go. You take whatever action you've been putting off.

In a stuck chapter of her own life, she used it to get herself to do even simple things: launching out of bed when her alarm went off in the morning and she'd rather hit snooze, starting the project she didn't want to start, making the phone call she knew she needed to make. And now millions of others have used the same rule to get themselves to take action on good, necessary, intimidating stuff.

This section is dedicated to the wake-up calls we all need to stop snoozing our way through if we're going to create interesting lives. It's chock full of reminders that our lives matter, that what we do with our time and our minds and our talents really matter, and we need to wake up, over and over. There are reminders to kick external validation out of the driver's seat, and to do what it takes to trust yourself and God more than anyone else.

In a busy age of human history, it can be easy to live even a good life on autopilot, never really daring, never really venturing, never really figuring out what you want and hope for. And in an AI future, it's going to matter even more that we catch ourselves when we're snoozing our way through life. We've got to catch ourselves when we start outsourcing our meaning or personal autonomy, then do something about it.

Ready to get out of bed, literally or figuratively? It's wake-up time for us to be dreamers who design their lives instead of letting life pass us by.

Who I Wrote This Book For

I wrote this book for who I used to be, for the dreamer at a desk or sitting restlessly on a cushion of ignored or yet-to-be-discovered dreams. It's for those who say they've forgotten how to dream, but were still drawn to this title. It's also for the ones who are trying to make their dreams happen but feel stuck or discouraged. It's for those who compare themselves to traditional high achievers and feel like they should be "responsible" like them. Who says it's irresponsible to take a chance on something you feel in your bones is right, will work out, or be worthwhile in the long run?

This book is for anyone with that restlessness in your soul that's telling you there's more for you, that you are only scratching the surface of your potential. You've got aspirations and ideas and things of your own you want to do. Languages you want to learn, advanced degrees leading to new career paths, major career pivots you've been talking about making, products you want to invent, businesses you want to start, books you want to write, things you want to paint, races you want to train for and run, and latent talents to develop while we're here in this fabulous life.

You know, the things we all say we'll do if we had more time. Or money. Or were more confident or prettier or less stressed or didn't need the benefits provided through your healthcare provider, were skinnier or less tired or... the list can go on and on. And usually does.

I wrote this book for those of you who aren't even sure what it is you want. You just know you wonder what it'd be like to seek out something on your own instead of just accepting what comes your way. When you don't start exploring to see what's even in that heart of yours, the worst part about staying stuck happens, and that is that you can start believing that it's too late. Or that you really are this version of yourself. Or that maybe there isn't anything you actually want out of life, or that you shouldn't want anything beyond the life you already have.

But no matter how accurately your specific situation is captured thus far, this much I know: If you picked up a book titled *Dear Fellow Dreamer* and made it this far, this book is for you. I wrote it for you. We are definitively dreamer friends and I can't wait to see what you discover in it uniquely for you.

You're Not Malcontent, You're Just Ready for More

You're never going to be content walking for your entire life if flying is in your soul.

Until the day you die, that niggling feeling that you weren't meant to just walk will tug at you. Not because you're malcontent, but because you were meant for something different than what you're comfortable doing.

If everyone just made the best of their first job or the first business they stumbled into, there would never be the critical interruptions to careers and personal development and companies and the economy.

We're meant to be dissatisfied, learn from that experience, and do something about it.

A Memorable Life

Very few places are famous just because they exist. Some are famous because they're extraordinarily beautiful, others because they're extreme or stark or wild. But we typically remember places where significant things happened. Where people were changed, where things didn't just continue in unabated ease.

Ronda, Spain, which, due to my inability to roll my r's, I cannot pronounce as romantically as it warrants, is famous for its beauty, its location on the edges of ginormous cliffs, and its historicity.

And the fact that writers and artists throughout the centuries visited and did their artistic things there.

It was just any other beach until it was chosen for the landing of...

It was just a mountain until...

It was just an empty desert until...

It was just an ordinary cathedral until...

It was just a small town until...

Famous isn't the goal, but a memorable-to-you life might be.

Stop Dismissing Your Inspiration

The estimable Ralph Waldo Emerson was a fan of personal autonomy. Or self-reliance, to use his vernacular. In his essay by the same name, he said this:

> "A man should learn to detect and watch that gleam of light which flashes across his mind from within, more than the lustre of the firmament of bards and sages. Yet he dismisses without notice his thought, because it is his. In every work of genius we recognize our own rejected thoughts: they come back to us with a certain alienated majesty. »[1]

Well, if that isn't a zinger. If we're going to live more awake to life and our dreams, we've got to start taking those gleams of light from within more seriously. That's where the work and creations of others you admire started, and the same will be true for you.

Lead Actor in Your Own Life

Good news: There is aspiration baked into *all* of us. It's the thing that makes every kid want to walk, to move. Well, except for two I'm thinking of who didn't seem all that interested in getting around. They did eventually muster enough drive to do more than sit, and grew up to be perfectly mobile and hopefully curious adults. And I guess I can think of a lot of adults who don't seem to have much aspiration. But that's not you or me, so onward we go.

That said, somewhere along the way even aspiring adults can settle into "good enough" or the corporate or entrepreneurial hustle of being so busy doing all the things. Media of all kinds and phones and digital courses are remarkably unhelpful on this front. With endless distraction we can feel like we really *did* something, when actually all we did was consume content, watch other people do cool things, talk about the things other people are doing, and dream about all the things we're going to do when we get more time.

It may feel hypocritical to mention something I've learned from a movie in the same breath that I'm suggesting we consume less, but there is a lot of the human experience packed into such things. My favorite college professor was fond of saying "God is willing to give us truth in whatever form we're willing to receive it." Frankly, I get a lot of truth out of movies—lines and scenes and beautiful experiences.

On an overnight flight into the Paris CDG airport, I stumbled across *The Holiday*. A line from Iris (Kate Winslet) leaped right off the 5.5x8 inch screen a mere nine inches from my face: "You're supposed to be the leading lady of your own life." That got scribbled in my notebook of ideas and treasures.

Boy, if that isn't the truth. Because if not you, who else on Earth can possibly fill that role? If you've taken on a supporting actor role in your own life story, or find yourself lurking at the edges of the stage, it's high time for a rewrite. You've just got to see what it's like at center stage, which does not mean that you turn selfish or superficial or self-absorbed. It just means you start using more of that gorgeous agency of yours to refine your interests and character, to love others more honestly, to make stuff happen. Literally no other person can be the leading lady or man of your life and do these things for you.

Let Go of Your Favorite Doorknob

Picture yourself in a hallway, holding the doorknob of one door. This door leads to a safe and familiar and very responsible and potentially very comfortable room where you've spent a lot of time. You know this room very well. It's where all your "shoulds" live.

Across the hall is another door you want to try. You sneaked a peek into it, and want to explore it and maybe spend some time there. Or maybe you don't actually know what's inside, but you're irresistibly drawn to it.

Here's the catch: The new doorknob is out of reach as long as you keep clinging to the one you know. The only way to open the new door—and many others—is to let go of the one you've been holding for a really long time.

Because mixing metaphors is fun, here's another take on it: You may not know or be able to fully commit to the right path, until you leave the one you've been hiking for a while now.

God might just be waiting for you to let go of what feels safe or familiar before putting wind into your sails for a new direction.

In a book I see as written to validate every dreamer who's tried many things or wants to try many things, *Range: Why Generalists Triumph in a Specialized World*, David Epstein introduces us to a floundering soul, a failed artist, art dealer, wanderer, teacher, awkward preacher, tutor, bookstore clerk. His name? Vincent Van Gogh. One of the most famous artists in the world was *twenty-seven* before he tried art again—after showing absolutely no talent for it as a child.

The Van Gogh Museum's website describes 1873–1881 of Van Gogh's life as "Looking for a direction."[2] But even after he found his direction and launched into painting, he didn't "make it" as an artist for some time. He was nearly thirty-three when critics told him he was no artist and that he actually belonged in the children's art class. He wrote to his brother, "[A man] doesn't always know himself what he could do, but he feels by instinct,

I'm good for something, even so!...I know that I could be quite a different man!...There's something within me, so what is it!"[3]

We could argue that he found that something within him, and so does every dreamer willing to wrestle for theirs.

You Didn't Come Here Just to Dream

Here's the thing:

You didn't come here to dream.

Correction: You didn't come here *just* to dream.

You came here to live, to expand, to soar, to feel the wind in your sails.

To be grateful for who and where you are, even though you want more.

Not more stuff or status, but more *living*.

To get all kinds of scuffed up by trying.

To have exhilarating moments of, "How does this get to be my life!?"

To feel lost and like you've lost your way.

To get found in wonder and spend time in curiosity.

To be grateful for the rutty roads that have brought you where you are.

But that gratitude isn't meant to immobilize you.

If your dreams are gifts—and they are—be grateful.

Then get busy doing things with and about them.

Even if you don't fully understand where it's all leading.

Because here's a fact: If you do nothing with your existing dreams and talents, you'll never unearth the buried ones.

And those might be the most beautiful of all.

Not Here to Mindlessly Blend In

You're not here to blend in. It's wild how something that comes so naturally to babies and toddlers—being wonderfully *you*—is something that becomes harder to do as adults. Especially in a social media world where we can mindlessly wear similar stuff, watch similar stuff, and drink water out of similar stainless steel containers. Never mind that most of us born before 1990 didn't even really *drink* water until that became a popular pastime in the twenty-first century.

As sketch artist and financial planner, Carl Richards, says, "Your Thing is uncovered by learning to be yourself."[4] Yes, Carl. And I'd add that sometimes Your Thing is what takes you on the exhilarating journey of learning to just be yourself. It's like what we in the biz call a cyclical relationship. One thing leads to another which leads to another which leads to another and I bet you get the point.

I don't want to be overly obvious here, but self-discovery is an inside job. No one can do it for you, and you can't think your way into it. It only happens as you go into The Unknown, do *some* introspecting, bump into new things and people, learn what you really like, and see what makes you wonderfully you. Even if that all ends up looking like lots of others, it's perfectly all right since different isn't necessarily the goal. Proven, self-discovered, and alive—that's where the real juice is.

It's Time to Blossom

> "And the day came when the risk to remain tight in a bud was more painful than the risk it took to blossom."
>
> Anais Nin

We Need Aims of Our Own

One of the most energizing places I've ever been was prison.

Several years ago, I was in a small, vacant parking lot outside the Utah State Prison, praying for help getting inside. Not a figurative prayer but a very literal one. And yes, I appreciate that this can't be a common occurrence *outside* prisons. But I was big-time nervous and didn't know what to do.

I had volunteered to teach a budgeting class to pre-parole inmates at the Utah State Prison. I knew from firsthand experience how limiting financial bondage could be, and I wanted to do something to help soon-to-be paroled inmates stay financially free as they re-entered society. I'd been through the mandatory orientation, received the requisite clearance, had my badge and the briefest of instructions for where to be and what to do when I arrived that first day.

Moments later, a prison employee pulled up next to me in the parking lot and helped me get inside. The volunteer coordinator eventually collected me from the waiting area, and we headed back toward the classroom area. As we entered a long hall seemingly swimming with men in white uniforms, I was overwhelmed by the sudden immersion in everything unfamiliar. Lots of things surprised me about that day. The thing that shocked me most was the unexpected and palpable feeling of *excitement*—of hope—which filled the halls. These guys were *awake*, y'all.

This feeling of aliveness was especially pronounced because it was a contrast to the vibe in the office building I'd left just an hour earlier. There, we corporate employees were technically free as birds, but the feeling of appreciation for freedom was much less pronounced than in prison. Go figure. It may have been a particularly low-energy day in the office, but considering that

I noticed this contrast more than once, I attribute some of the discrepancy to the fact that those men in prison had *plans*, y'all. They were each imagining and working toward something positive and definite and something their own.

It can be easy, in even uncomfortably comfortable situations, to coast or to be busy enough that your plans get deprioritized until they're a vague memory or far distant aims. One day, you say. One day I'm going to finish that novel I'm writing. Or one day I'm going to start a business and see what happens. One day I'm going to figure out how to meaningfully spend my time here on Earth.

How about you start being energized right now about taking good care of the freedom you already have? Start making the most of the time, dreams, money, and stuff you already have to set you up for where you want to go. And if you don't know what Your Thing is, an idea of *anything* of your own will do, as long as it's accompanied by action.

This Will Be All if You Don't Start Listening

You've perhaps also had stuck chapters where your most beautiful dreams feel impractical or just went really quiet while you focus on the life right in front of you. Instead of putting energy toward shaping your own future, taking chances, and figuring out what you want to build and grow, you find yourself doing more existing than really living.

But even in these chapters you also get fleeting feelings of "this isn't it" in the form of musings like "Is this all there is to my life?" The short answer to that question is a resounding no.

It will be, though, if you don't start taking your dreams and your potential more seriously than you take yourself and your fears.

Let The Music Out

According to Wayne Dyer's daughter, Serena, one of the main lessons she has learned from her spiritual father is: "Don't die with your music still in you."

What's your "music"? Perhaps it's actual music that you're not making or sharing widely. Maybe you're a very funny person, but you have told yourself you're shy and don't want to put yourself out there, even in conversation. Or you could be the person to make a real difference to teenagers with your unique experiences, but you're not doing anything about it, or your painting gift, or your books of poetry, or your vision to revitalize your hometown, or...the list could go on and on.

Without waxing too poetic—not my current genre—I see "the music" as what Elizabeth Gilbert describes in her book, *Big Magic*. You didn't necessarily ask for it to come to you, it just did. This creative muse that's come is giving you a chance to find the hidden treasures in you.

But you often don't get the full musical score at once, just a few notes here and there. The usual figure of speech is "I hate to break it to you," but I actually would *love* to break it to you that letting the music out means letting those flashes of creativity lead you into uncertainty and risk and all you'll learn by venturing.

News to no one—you're going to die one day. And it will be a real shame if the music only you can write—and which makes you more alive while you're here—dies with you.

Do You Like the Life You've Built?

Do you actually *like* the life you've built? Now is as good a time as any, and better than in twenty years, to ask that question. Or to get serious (in a fun way) about it, before AI possibly changes all of it, for better or worse.

Do you actually care about having the nicest house on the block? Do you even like the parties you're invited to or the things you talk about with friends and neighbors? Or all the things you attend or feel pressured to keep up with?

There's a scene I love in a rom-com of my college years, *Return to Me*. The main couple meets their hoity-toity friends at a gala. Said friends are bought in *hard* on status. They brag about their upcoming travel plans to Tuscany and ask the main character couple about their travel plans. David Duchovny's character responds in complete deadpan:

"We're thinking about going to one of those themed water parks for the weekend."

My kind of people.

So back to you: Do you genuinely like the life and work you're creating? Will you like it long-term? I hope so. And if you don't, it's not too late to set about changing it.

The Point of Dreams

What's the whole point of pursuing your dreams? It's not about fame or status or power or being extraordinary. You can pursue those other things and call them your dream, but they don't count as cherished aspirations. Aspirations, yes. Cherished, no.

Exploring and following your dreams is about creating and being more of yourself and not just acting a tiny bit like everybody else. More creativity and more of our potential reached is what we all want deep down, especially us principled dreamers. I imagine most parents want their kids to be themselves, and not an amalgamation of the kids in their classrooms.

Discovering and pursuing your dreams means you're doing something that is so authentically *you* and it's going to lead somewhere wonderful. My grandpa loved making stuff like furniture and engines and contraptions. He never sold any of things or got famous for them except for in the Quartzsite, Arizona, retirement community parade; he simply loved making things, so he did.

Here's another riff on it: I personally believe God sent us here to be ourselves and to make the most of our potential. And the only way we find out who we are is by doing the hard, stretching, wonderful, amazing things that might look risky to others. It's in the wrestle that we get closest to our Creator.

It only took me a few hours of a twelve-week improv class to start to learn this. What authentically bubbles up in us and gets shared is much more beautiful, interesting, funny, and connecting than anything we manufacture to try and get a specific response from.

Comfort zones, whether in a job, a business, or a relationship, can reward conformity to who you've been to other people, to maintaining status quo, to going along with more pretending than you may know. I don't blame the comfort zones or the people in them; sometimes we all need to rest there. And some people have no problem spending their whole life in theirs. But if you're reading this book, comfort zones don't work for you, or they don't work for you anymore.

Whether you're contemplating a leap or are in the messy middle of making a go of things, here's your PSA to wake up...to being *you*.

Don't Be the Musical Where Nothing Happens

Let's talk about a musical I saw on Broadway recently: The lights go down, the orchestra starts playing enthusiastically, and the curtain lifts to reveal an absolutely stunning scene. The entire cast including the hero and heroine eventually dance and sing their way onto the stage, the audience claps enthusiastically, and the opening scene ends. Then guess what happens? Well not much.

There's some more singing and dancing, people say some nice things to each other, and the stage set gets rearranged sometimes, but there's no villain, there's no quest, or really any character progression for any of the characters.

If you haven't figured it out, I'm making up this entire musical. I did actually see an incredible Broadway musical—*Wicked*—just after The Boat Journey of 2023. The set, the score, the dancing, and the costumes were fabulous. But what made it so great was the people and the story and the quests and failures and progressions of each character.

Without plot, we'd all be passing time, and there's only so much of that we can do. In another musical, *Shrek*, there's a song called "I Know It's Today" where an increasingly jaded princess sings about "the waiting, the waiting, the *waiting*." She's of course waiting for her Prince Charming to arrive and deliver her from a life of boredom.

Imagine your life as a stage-worthy musical: There's a whole audience of people—a big one of family and friends from the past, present, and future—who love you and can't wait to see what you do and become. There's an amazing stage set (hello, Planet Earth!) and some pretty fabulous costume options and all kinds of figurative and literal theme music you can choose from.

But the quest and the character progression? Well, that's up to you and to God and to what you discover as you make some moves. What will your quests be that elicit tears and laughter and raucous applause along the way from those who love you most, certainly including yourself? Picture yourself at center stage, acting or dancing or writing or leading or serving or creating your heart out.

Triple-dog dare you to write and live *this* sort of musical instead of the waiting, plotless sort of musical. Center stage, not the wings, is where your best stuff happens. It's where you at least give magic a chance of happening, whether things work out exactly as or when you think they should.

Neon Signs It's Time to Grow

Restlessness, not resolved by enriching your present life, is a sign that it's time for growth.

So is your persistent and principled desire to leave or close a chapter you once loved.

And on the other end of the spectrum, your complacency—a feeling that "everything's fine"—is a *big* ol' neon sign that everything is not actually good.

It's time to grow.

You Can't Outspend a Life You Don't Like

In my experience, we tend to overspend—time and money—when we don't like our lives. It's way easier to buy a new outfit or over-consume Netflix and get a crummy substitute of a feeling like we're doing something interesting than it is to create something, to sacrifice some comfort for growth, to figure out how we actually want to be spending our time.

You can't outspend a life you don't like. You also can't spend your way into one you love. Much of our spending is an attempt to fill the gaping holes in a soul meant to hope and dream. Your soul goes with you at the end, but the material stuff gets left behind. All of our overspending is akin to feeding our body movie theater popcorn and Oreos for dinner when it's begging for vegetables and actual sustenance. Nothing wrong in my book with occasional popcorn and Oreos, but they're a lame substitute for what your body actually wants and needs.

You can distract yourself for years by furnishing and decorating a home, curating your fantasy sports team, taking courses, picking out paint colors, maintaining all that stuff you've bought, looking for just the right platter for entertaining. All while your dreams go stale on the shelves. But a dreamer can only distract themselves from a stuck life for so long. I suspect AI is, sooner or later, going to force every last one of us to get unstuck anyway, so we might as well get busy making it our choice. Here's to spending our time and money in ways that lead to more—more *living* and more *life*.

Out From Under a Rock

Sometimes the only way to discover yourself or eventually be discovered doing the thing you love, is by doing something about any one of your dreams or talents or passions. But they can usually only find you if you're already doing something in the neighborhood of the things you dream of doing.

You've got to believe in your thing enough to make your own moves. Which may put you in positions to be "discovered" or found by people who might just be looking for someone making or offering stuff or solutions like you uniquely are.

No one discovers that you're wonderful if you live under a figurative rock, or a literal one for that matter. Or if you never share your thing with the world, waiting to get permission or for someone else to remove every stone and log from the path between you and it.

Plus, that would 1000% defeat the purpose of a dream, your potential, and your gift of agency. The whole point of wanting to do something, and then doing something about it, is that you're going to get really scuffed up and creative about trying to move forward on the trail toward it. This journey is where you start to really discover what you are made of and what you deeply care about. And if you ask me, that's the most exciting result of all.

It doesn't work to live well beneath your potential and wonder why you're not achieving it.

Most People Sell Themselves Short

Well if this doesn't wake all of us right up.

> "The story of the human race is the story of men
> and women selling themselves short."
>   Abraham Maslow

Let's stop selling ourselves short.

They Started Just Like You and Me

Aren't you glad your favorite people dreamed? And that your favorite creators and inventors and leaders and athletes *did* something about their dreams?

For every single manmade thing we enjoy, someone had to have a thought. Probably a whole tangled mess of thoughts, but one persisted or emerged as a gleam of inspiration.

And then they had to think that maybe, just maybe, they could do something with or about that thought. They had to believe that they could learn the things they needed to, or refine a talent or passion to bring it into the world, then actually *do* it through all the hard and the self-doubt and the failures and the close calls and the sleepless nights and the financial stress.

And for many of them, what we best know them for is not what they even set out to do. They had to *earn* those best ideas by taking action and trying stuff and failing publicly and repeatedly on any one of their ideas. They'd never have otherwise bumped into some of the most memorable and interesting ideas we all appreciate.

Inspirational Late Bloomers

Here's a dose of late-blooming dreamers to encourage us all:

Toni Morrison didn't write her first novel until she was forty, and did so while working as an editor at Random House. She received a Pulitzer Prize at fifty-six.

Stan Lee, the gentleman who went on to create the itty-bitty franchise we know today as the Marvel Universe, didn't have his first hit comic until he was almost thirty-nine.

Martha Stewart, one of the most well-known names in home-making, became famous at forty-one with the release of her first book. Her company, Martha Stewart Living, didn't even form until seven years after that. And time in prison didn't slow her growth, which is just proof that there's a lot of room for mistakes in life. This is not me recommending you do illegal things, it's just a lesson for all of us to forgive ourselves for our less egregious mistakes.

Vera Wang, of wedding dress fame, didn't even enter the fashion industry until she was forty. Who knew that before that she was a journalist and a figure skater?

The couple who started Gap didn't do so until he was forty, and they had no experience with retail. Can you even imagine malls around America without Gap?

Julia Child was fifty before her first cookbook was published.

Samuel L. Jackson didn't start making it big in movies until age forty-three, in the late 1980s, and didn't have his big break until 1994. Guess what year he started acting? In the 1970s. His IMDB biography page calls his *Pulp Fiction* breakthrough as "going from supporting player to leading man."[5]

And how about this one? Laura Ingalls Wilder didn't publish her first book until she was *sixty-five*. She didn't even start writing until her mid-forties, which makes me feel all kinds of ahead of the game. The success of her popular *Little House on the Prairie* books means even more to this dreamer knowing now that she didn't have an easy row to hoe in her adult life. Laura and her husband had barns and homes burn down, crops destroyed, battles with diphtheria, and multiple moves to where it seemed like things might be better.[6] It reads like something right from the early computer game, Oregon Trail.

Whatever your dream is and however old you are, it's not too late and you're not behind. Everyone of these late bloomers inspires us to dare and tackle new things our whole lives. And reminds us that some of our very favorite creations are still ahead, yet to be discovered.

Life is Now, Not a Horizon

I see you. Going about the business of living, and doing a wonderful job of it. Making plans, volunteering, making friends with strangers, trying to take care of your health, your people, yourself.

You sometimes don't feel like enough.

You have high standards for yourself, and can be hard on yourself.

You're happy, but think deep down you'll be at least a teensy bit happier when you have more time or money or get married or you have the kids you've always wanted or the kids are older or you have more financial security or status.

I get this general space. We all spend time there.

Staring out the window, daydreaming of adventure.

Making plans.

Wishing you had *more* plans.

Wishing you had *fewer* plans.

Wanting to have time to read all the books you've acquired.

Wanting to be more needed, more connected, more occupied.

Feeling *too* occupied.

Eating breakfast and remembering that you don't actually like eggs very much. But, hey—protein.

Cleaning up breakfast/lunch/dinner/snacks. Over and over and over. For those of you unloading dishwashers every single day, you have my admiration.

Deciding when to eat meals, what to have, what not to have...

Flossing.

Watching Netflix.

Exercising.

Trying to declutter your space.

Stressing about your job, your business, your income.

Reading.

Thinking. Oh, the thinking!

This is it, folks. The real deal. There is no moment at which we say "Ah ha! Now life has begun." Whatever it looks like right now, this is your life.

And it's all good. And, in the spirit of improv, let's tack an "and" on the party. Maybe even two for fun.

Try this: "Yes, this is my life *and* I choose to be grateful for it. *And* I also want to simplify my life where possible so I can do something about any one of my dreams."

You don't know when you're going to meet your love, but you can know that you want to love your life. Meeting each other will be sweeter if you both have chosen to love your lives and to do something about your dreams.

You are never going to know exactly what you're doing with your life. Or if you do, you might be thinking too small. But you can have a general contentment about your life and direction and know what you're going to do to live meaningfully *today*—and how you're going to make your tomorrows rich in the ways that matter. And while we never know the difference we've made in the lives of others, we can try to make a difference for one person today.

Stages of Behavior Change

There's a fancily named thing called the "Transtheoretical Model of Change" in which scientists James Prochaska and Carlo Di-Clemente observed stages of, you guessed it—you smart person you—change. Particularly behavior changes. They were trying to make sense of why some smokers were able to quit smoking on their own, while others couldn't or didn't. Their conclusion sounds remarkably simple, but holy smokes have I seen it play out over and over in financial coaching. That conclusion? People change negative behaviors if they're ready to change.[7] Yup, there it is—truth.

Here are their stages for your reviewing pleasure. Along with my own commentary—this is my book after all. I get to say stuff.

1. **Pre-contemplation**. At this stage, we have no plan to take action because we don't see problems as problems. We might make excuses for why things are the way they are, or, my personal favorite, blame others. We might be real defensive at this stage.

But it's okay—it's still part of the change process and has to precede the next stage.

2. **Contemplation**. At this stage, we know we need to make changes to have the life we want, but we're not sure *what* to do and are still getting sold on the whole idea. According to one source, there's a lack of confidence, a lack of sureness about actually wanting the change.[8] In a real wake-up call to dreamers everywhere, this same source indicates that "It might take as little as a couple weeks or as long as a lifetime to get through the contemplation stage." Whoa ho ho. A lifetime?! Does anyone want to spend their *entire* lifetime just thinking about making changes that can unlock *life*—and never making those changes? I can safely say I don't, and you don't either—you're reading a book called *Dear Fellow Dreamer* for crying out loud.

3. **Preparation**. We're now *getting ready* to make a change. We're getting ready to quit things we know aren't helpful, or start doing things that will improve our lives, but not taking action quite yet. You're researching and unearthing the information you need so that the actions you start taking in the next stage can last. Interestingly, this is the phase most people skip. They jump right to action. In making a lasting money behavior change, this is the "unsexy" pre-budgeting stage that most people want to skip. But it's also where risk-averse dreamers in comfortable jobs can get stuck. Or where even "messy middle" entrepreneurs can get stuck—consuming endless information about the thing they're eventually going to do. It's entirely possible to spend years planning and never get around to any real doing.

4. **Action**. According to the surprisingly sexy book *Facilitating Financial Health*,[9] this stage "is often the shortest of all stages."

This magical stage is where you *do* something about the thing you've been getting ready to do. This is also where willpower kicks in and where you become the most likely to accept influence from others.

5. **Maintenance**. This is where the change sticks or gets tweaked. I love this stage for me, and for you. This is what you get when you embrace each stage, including the preparation stage.

Which stage are you and your dreams in?

No One Can Know Your Dreams For You

Be careful about getting sold a dream that isn't your own.

No one but you can know what your dreams are. Others can't know what things you uniquely feel compelled to create.

They can't tell you what you want.

They can only guess at it.

They can see native proclivities and strengths you might be missing.

But *you've* got to start seeing your strengths, or you'll never have the guts to go into the unknowns of dreaming and building .

That said, I have a spoiler alert for you: Some of your biggest strengths you won't see until you leap and spend time in the messy middle. And if you keep just taking the opportunities that come to you, you might never actually figure out what *you* actually want.

There was a moment several years ago when I realized I was hoping to be discovered—like, someone would see my talent, or know what I'd really enjoy, and pin a rose on my nose while saying, "You're just what we need at this time."

Here's the thing: People do get discovered. We hear about people being discovered by a casting director or music magnate or sports scout or a writer gets their big break when a publisher or literary agent sees something marvelous in their book proposal or 108th Substack essay. Phyllis Smith is better known now as Phyliss Vance, married to Bob Vance of Vance Refrigeration in the TV show, *The Office*. She was a casting assistant when someone offered her the role of Phyllis, a role she was made for.

But while she was discovered out of her casting assistant role, we've got to appreciate that she was already in the figurative neighborhood of something she wanted to be discovered for. It's a rare case that someone wasn't doing a dang thing about their dream or curiosity and someone came to their home to say, "You know what? I think you'd really love *volleyball*. Have you ever thought about playing, and can I make volleyball success happen for you?" And they do, you love it, and it becomes the dream you didn't even dare to dream or know you had.

Cases like this are a serious exception. And while none of us would be opposed to them, the real magic—and the magic we have the most control over—occurs in taking steps toward the thing you want, perfectly fine knowing that the thing may end up changing or simply being a vehicle to bring you to a place where you meet new versions of yourself and your potential.

Sure, you might get "discovered" at work and be offered a promotion. Or, in your entrepreneurial efforts, someone *may* offer you opportunities that flatter you or are financially enticing. But these opportunities may not be what you actually want for your life. And even if they are, do you really want to wait for someone else to just hand you an interesting life?

Your Potential Is Getting Squished

What does this look like for you and me? Well, a modern, first-world life of getting and acquiring and earning and spending and managing possessions and observing others do the same thing, does a marvelous job of absolutely trapping our potential in materialism. Kind of like how Michelangelo's sculptures were, according to him, already formed and just buried by superfluous marble.

Consumption is the default state for most of us. It's not bad to own or want a lovely home, have nice cars, and wear nice clothes. But when those things come between you and your gorgeous potential, we do have a real problem.

If we're so busy getting and maintaining stuff, our unique personalities and souls can easily get buried under a steady and superfluous barrage of minutiae. The point of life isn't to have the most or nicest stuff. You might end up getting cool things and becoming rich along the way, and if you do it thoughtfully, those things won't ruin your life. But the point for dreamers is to grow into who you were meant to be, to become more of you than you already are. To think beautiful thoughts, to create beautiful things, to learn, to expand.

For his birthday, one of my nephews asked for "those animals that grow in water." I sent him what ended up being a lifetime supply from Amazon. You know the kind—a foam animal compressed into a capsule which dissolves in water. Some dreamers are squished into figurative capsules. These might take the form of a literal cubicle or a figurative one where you're only a small portion of the real you. But when you add water—intentional action and planning and belief—you can grow into a wonderfully magnified version of yourself.

There may be things you are already dabbling in, but only dabbling in. Half-started passion projects you plan to get to one day when you have more time or when life calms down. Or you might be acting real busy in your creative work, but getting nowhere. Or you have known talents you keep putting off developing because it's just easier to keep the existing dynamic of life in motion, or because it seems like a lot of work to get your painting stuff out when you're not sure why it's important that you do.

And then there are the latent things in you that you have yet to discover. Things you will actually love doing, that will bring your soul to life, that will give you that passion for waking up that people talk about.

But, they'll stay hidden in figurative marble until you get intentional about finding them, about surfacing them, about chiseling away at the *busyness* of life to reveal them. In my experience, these dreams only surface while you're taking action on any idea of yours, and most often you can't think your way into them. Journaling and thinking about what you want out of life is helpful, but too much of that keeps a dreamer from the business of actual living.

Your words written down, your dreams acted upon, your products invented, your goals worked toward, your experiences lived out, these all make room for what's waiting to come next; the next round, the deeper layers, the richness that life is going to bring you if you stay engaged in trying to live a substantial life. Your best stuff is not in your head; it's in your heart. And the only way you bring to the surface what's there is to take vigorous action on any creative idea that is already in your head and begin to unearth that gorgeous potential of yours.

People Need You

Why on earth would you leave a perfectly good comfort zone to head into The Unknown? Or do unknown things in service of expanding your comfort zone?

Well, how about because people need who you are and who you're going to become as you engage with life. Your gifts are meant to be discovered and shared freely, after all. Specific people need *you* specifically to do more than stay in your comfy sweats on the couch watching Netflix. Nothing wrong with sweats, couches, or Netflix—just not as a main mode of life.

Not everyone currently has the feeling that there's something more for them to be doing in life. If you're reading a book like this one, you do, and you're meant to listen. Other people will hopefully have this feeling at some point in their lives, and maybe you'll be part of helping them get there. Since you, however, are already having it, it's time to listen. It's not your job to know who your talents are going to inspire, reach or bless; it's just your job to not hide them at home. They'll take it from there.

Speaking of talents, do you know the Parable of the Talents from the Bible? For the uninitiated, here's how it goes: A rich master distributes talents to his servants. One guy receives five talents, another receives two, and the last one gets one talent. Eventually, the master comes back and asks for an accounting of their talent development program. The first guy doubled his five, and is rewarded with five more. The second guy doubled his two, and is similarly rewarded with another two. But the lord is not *at all* happy with the last guy who, out of fear, buried his single talent for fear of losing it. He loses it all right; the master takes the talent he was so afraid of losing and gives it to the guy with ten—that guy really *appreciated* his talents.

What if your favorite artists or musicians or composers or poets had relegated their work to just napkin scratches that no one would ever see? Life would be pretty dang drab without the creative works and innovations and accomplishments of those who tried to do something with their talents, and those who went after the ones they wanted to have.

Don't "Do Your Dream Wrong"

The only way you get your dream wrong is by "doing it wrong."

As in, if someone causes offense or injury to another, we would say they "did them wrong." Are you offending your dreams by doubting them, dismissing them, or ignoring them altogether?

You Have Three Choices Right Now

Whenever we're in a dissatisfactory situation, we've all got the same three basic options. Sure, there are an infinite number of sub-options, but we don't have time for that. We're keeping it simple, like at In-N-Out where you get to choose between one patty or two, cheese or no cheese, and "animal style" which does *not* mean the same thing everywhere no matter what everyone else tells me.

Our menu options for dealing with our life situations are as follows:

Improve them.

Accept them.

Make a change.

And sometimes you have to a) try to **improve** something, *anything*, about the situation or yourself in it before you can b) **accept** it for what it is, and c) be ready to **make an exciting change** of your own instead of hoping for the situation to change on its own.

Sometimes it does and there are things we learn in the waiting and the delays, but most often one of these three options is available to us to make our circumstances more satisfactory.

Every Bird Has to Leave the Nest Eventually

At some point in every bird's life, it's time to fly.

I have no idea how birds are kicked out of their nests, and if this were a different type of book, I would spend days researching such a phenomenon. It's something most of us just *know*. Baby birds have to leave their nests to learn that they do, in fact, know how to fly.

But we grown-ups can sure come to love a comfy nest, even if it's only comfy because it's familiar.

Just like baby birds, though, we were never meant to live forever in nests.

Unlike baby birds, we may not have a mama bird kicking us out. Or, we might, but I always preferred to leave comfy nests on my own terms. So when are you going to leave whatever your comfy nest is?

Sometimes things *not* changing is your cue to change.

Sometimes the *nest* changing is your cue to make a move.

Sometimes it's that you know the only way your wings are going to figure out flying is if you leave a nest you've outgrown.

Sometimes it's all of the above.

And without question, finding that you're going backward is a definite cue to leave.

Every risk you take, even while in the nest, is a test flight to try out your wings.

To find the muscles you still needed to strengthen.

To discover the habits and mindsets that need tuning up.

To start contemplating new places and new possibilities where your wings might take you, since it turns out wings were not designed just for visual effect.

The Whole Point of Getting Ready Is to Go

You can only get ready for so long.

The whole point of getting ready is to be ready *enough* to actually start doing the thing.

Doing Nothing is Not the Goal

The goal of life is not to phone it in or work your way to doing nothing. There is no race to the retirement finish line or to the biggest pile of money or the emptiest calendar. The purpose of life is to, well, live. And perhaps the most accurate measure of a wealthy life is the spark in your eyes about what you're working on, learning, or contributing.

Two years of travel introduced me to all sorts of people, including a handful of FIRE (Financial Independence Retire Early) folks. The youngest FIRE individual I met was a guy in his thirties. I don't know much about his and his fiancee's journey to retirement, or how much they enjoyed the journey or how deep their roots were. All I know is that, when I asked him what he and his fiancee did with their time, it sounded like they mostly hung out—visiting family and friends, lots of beach time. She was dabbling in some business something she didn't seem very excited about and his main pastime seemed to be coasting through life.

It could be that this couple is just figuring out their next moves and what energizes them and, gosh, I sure hope so. Because aimlessly "hanging out" for several decades sounds pretty dang dreary. My post-corporate years of exploration and talking with people in a dozen countries has solidly convinced me that the goal of life is definitely *not* to not work. The point of life is not even to travel, even though I hope to do plenty more of it. In his book, *Amusing Ourselves to Death*, Neil Postman makes the case that amusement and ease are not the aims of life; we wreck ourselves and society when we pretend it is and orient everything around entertainment.

With all the possibilities of disruption courtesy of AI, it's never been more essential for dreamers to find ways to keep doing the things humans have always done to live meaningfully: enjoy solving problems, think deeply, be needed and stretched, maintain personal autonomy, and try to contribute to society and those around us.

Doing nothing was never the point of life.

Someday Isn't Guaranteed

The things you want to be able to do someday start now. Physician and author of the book *Outlive: The Science and Art of Longevity*, Peter Attia, asks his patients what they want to be able to do with a long life. He would say (and I would agree) that living a long, healthy and thriving life is far more desirable than just living a long time.

He tells his patients that if they want to hike, they better start, or keep, hiking now. If, at eighty, they want to be able to get out of a chair without effort, they'd better be building those muscles now. If they want to be able to lift heavy things, they'd better be lifting heavy things now.

But beyond physical health, what do you plan and hope to have or do Someday? Read? Learn new things? Pick up a sport? Travel with friends? Adventure outside? Volunteer? Start a business? As none of us are guaranteed a Someday, it seems like we'd better be doing something Today about some of the things we hope to get around to.

In my faith, we believe that we live—body and soul reunited—forever after our life on Earth. And that the quality of life we live forever is heavily influenced by our desires and choices here.

It's *almost like* our choices for our bodies and minds and souls matter. And that a growth trajectory is the most recommendable attitude to have throughout our lives.

I heard a retired, successful septuagenarian talk about his study of the French language and how he's never been to France. "Someday," he says. I'm sure he has very valid excuses for not going yet, but I sure hope he gets there before it's too late for him. I hear Paris is not to be missed. My luggage-laden sprint between Paris train stations as a seventeen-year-old doesn't count, and neither do multiple layovers in the CDG airport; it remains on my Someday list as well. But I'm not talking about it like he is.

2

PERMISSION SLIPS

Remember hall passes from school years? These golden tickets gave responsible students official sanction to do the thing they were doing. You know, exciting things like going to your locker or the bathroom. They preemptively protected you from hall monitors wanting to penalize you for being in the halls while everyone else was dutifully in class. That feeling of sanctioned freedom was hard to beat.

As adults, we dreamers can, at times, feel stuck in figurative, and I suppose literal, classrooms, longing for a permission—a hall pass—to act on our dreams and figuratively wander the halls. The good, but sometimes overwhelming, news is that *you* are the hall pass boss in your own life. You also might be the hardest to convince of the legitimacy of your plans.

Surrounded as we are by lovely people who thrive on security and responsibility and five-year-plans which you'd better believe they'll make happen, we dreamers can doubt our intuition. Wanting something different for ourselves, wanting to and being willing to take risks, to do things that don't always make sense but we trust will come to good—these can feel irresponsible or nonsensical. Like an invalid reason to leave the classroom.

If you tell a "responsible" person that you're a little fuzzy how exactly your endeavor is going to go, but that you trust it's going to be great, an opportunity for growth, and is leading somewhere amazing? They look at you with some serious "poor dear, you'd better get back to class" energy. They feel *much* better about things when they know you've got a definite plan and a guarantee of success for your creative venture, new business, or ridiculous goal.

But this portion of the book isn't about others. It's about you. And you giving yourself permission to dream those dreams and to prioritize your inner scaffolding over external supports. To listen to your intuition more than you listen to those who weren't given the same abilities to dream. Remember: The world *needs* intrepid souls willing to explore and dream and try stuff and fail and keep trying. Others will happily give their permission when it all works out.

Who Said You Had to Know?

It's okay not to know. That's how loads of people have done incredibly interesting things. I'm with Jerry Seinfeld on this one:

> "The less secure and confident you feel in the direction, the more surprises and excitement you

will have in store. That's good... The better the
job you've done in finding a path for yourself, the
more boring and predictable your life is going to
be."[10]

There are all kinds of corners in a life filled with dreams and
longings, and you're not expected to see around all of them.
The key to exploring and discovering new things is *not* knowing. We go new places and try new things precisely *because*
they're new to us and we don't know what we're going to find
there.

As a high school student, I went to see the movie *Truman Show*
which, as it turns out, is *not* about the 33rd President of the
United States. It's instead about a guy who unwittingly has
lived his entire life in a literal bubble with every moment and
relationship of his life crafted by a film studio.

He dreams of exploring, but everyone around him—paid ac-
tors masquerading as his friends and family—try to convince
him that life is best on Seahaven Island. They even manufacture
experiences to keep him from leaving. Miraculously, he remains
undaunted in his dreams of exploring in general, and going to
Fiji specifically to find his high school crush.

Sylvia was the only person in Truman's life who told him
the truth that everything in his world was fake. "Everyone's
pretending for you," she says. For this, she's removed from
the show under the pretext that the family is moving to Fiji.
Everything around him is indeed fake, and years after Sylvia first
tipped him off, Truman begins to see his reality for what it is.

In one scene, he skips work and decides to take his wife on a spontaneous road trip, destination unknown. Trying to talk him out of one option, Meryl asks why he would even want to go to Atlantic City when he hates gambling.

"Because I never have. That's why people go places."

It sure is—literally and figuratively.

When Is It My Turn?

It's your turn right now...

To practice gratitude.

To believe it's working out.

To listen to yourself.

To smile broadly.

To get ready for the day.

To walk like you know where you're heading.

To change your mind.

To not share more than you want to share.

To have your own back right this moment.

To try again tomorrow.

You Are Not the Only One

You have all the permission in the world to feel the way you feel. Stomach in your throat moments signal you're simply doing something new. These feelings just come with brave territory.

Literally *everyone* who is a) not an egomaniac and b) creating something worthwhile feels the exact same way at times, especially the ones for whom "success" is taking longer.

Don't You Dare Dismiss It

It's in your heart for a reason. And you'll know why one day.

Not All Who Wander Are Lost...

As a well-known quote from the trilogy *Lord of the Rings* goes:

> "Not all who wander are lost.
> All that is gold does not glitter,
> Not all those who wander are lost;
> The old that is strong does not wither,
> Deep roots are not reached by the frost."

The poem is about Aragon, the hunky ranger who spends his days seemingly wandering hither and thither. But it's not actually wandering; he has a purpose and a destiny, and his unconventional path through life is part of something bigger. He's not been sloppily vagabonding his way through life. No, no, no. He's been honing his skills, his intuition, and being refined as he walks the road less traveled. Getting those deep roots, you know.

If that doesn't just inspire the socks right off you and me, I don't know what will.

Permission to Want

One of the bravest things you can do is want. Not live *in* want, but know there's something different or more that you want. And being willing to do something about it.

If you're reading this book, you will understand a vague sense that there are things for you to be doing that don't necessarily involve your own comfort. This sense gets squashed pretty easily by thoughts like "Who you kidding, Kid? Who are you to think you can do something big? Who are you to call yourself a _____? Only people who get special permission slips get to be or do _____." Or how about this one: "You should just be happy where you are; you've got a great life."

I hereby give you permission to want something other than what you have. If you never wanted anything different, you'd never have left home, learned new things, moved cross country. Wanting takes you places.

Sometimes, you've spent a long, lame time wanting only what other people want, which yields a third-rate version of the life you're meant to be living. Sometimes, you legitimately want what other people want and discount your wanting because it feels like you're just being a copycat to say things like, "What I actually want is to also _____ or be a _____ or go _____."

Some really fun self-doubt can kick in at this point to tell you that you, in fact, can't want it. Others can, but you? Naw. Self-doubt might also get really practical and tell you you have to make a bunch of money first. Or that no one actually makes a living off writing or painting or dancing or singing or studying the habits and habitats of snails. And even if you actually know like five people just off the top of your head who do, *you* can't.

Or, the Want Judge kicks in and tells you that you shouldn't want that. That it's selfish or superficial, even if you know deep down you're not doing it for selfish or superficial reasons. I think you know that the kind of wanting I'm talking about—not the "I want to be ten pounds lighter" or "I want a new SUV" variety. I'm talking about wanting to create things and learn new talents and stretch yourself—for yourself, for God, for the chance at growth and for the hopeful result.

In case you need some reasons beyond explicit permission to want, here are a couple to consider:

If you don't let yourself want in the first place, you never get a chance to refine your wants or get at the root of your longings.

It's the path of least resistance to *not* want. It's much easier and certainly safer to *not* want, to *not* dream. Because if you don't ever want anything you can never be disappointed. You never fail or get bruised or embarrassed or disappoint yourself or fall short or feel the major dissonance caused by wanting something you're doing nothing about or even the friction of knowing you're being a pansy about your big wants.

But here's the thing. When you want and want big, then match it with action, things have a way of working out, sometimes in ways we could not have even imagined.

And it's why I'll continue to insist loudly that wanting—dreaming—is one of the bravest and most important things we humans do. Part of wanting is signing yourself up to be disappointed if things don't work out. Heck, *when* things don't work out; things not working out is part and parcel of having dreams and daring to do something about them.

Your Risk Tolerance is a Gift

God gave dreamers a higher than average tolerance for risk.

What if He wants you to explore the gift and use it while you're here?

Prioritize Your Interests

Remarkable things can happen when you let yourself prioritize the things you've always wanted to do.

The last time I had roommates, I had some of the very best. For one of our escapades—we called it I Spy Pie Night—I made a lemon meringue pie and off we went for the "I Spy" portion of the night. For some time we'd been wanting to stake out a local strip club. You know, to see what kind of people frequent such an establishment and we didn't even know what else.

Dressed in all black, the three of us parked across the street from the club. We slunk down in the seats of Anne's SUV and took turns peering through the binoculars to narrate—colorfully—for the others what we observed. After nearly an hour of that party, we went home, had pie, and called it a fun night. But as interesting as all this is, I didn't come here to tell you all about the fun we made as roommates. I came here to tell you about Nicole, one of the adventuresome roommates.

This inspiration of a woman is one goal-oriented and goal-achieving powerhouse. While we were roommates, she worked as a pediatric charge nurse, dated lots, had a busy social life and many important things to do with her roommates. Despite this full plate, she also made more progress in a single year on her goals than I had even *conceived* in the preceding five years.

See, Nicole had a binder.

In said binder, she had a list of life goals.

The first three entries on her long list were:

1. Learn to play the violin.

2. Run a marathon.

3. Write a book.

Guess what she did during the year of our flatmate-ship?

She took violin lessons and practiced. Poorly, I might add—but that's simply where everyone starts when they're doing something new.

She trained for and ran a marathon.

She figured she should start her creative writing journey with a creative writing course, and was actively completing that during our roommate tenure. Then she wrote her book, a fantasy novel, and published it. Then she wrote *seventy* more, within ten years. Seventy!

Remember how Nicole set out to write *one* book? Even if she secretly planned to write more, I'm positive she did not set out to write seventy-and-counting books. But this is just the sort of thing that can just sort of happen when you give yourself permission to start simply and do something—anything—about the things on your own life goal list.

A Leap Out of Practical

On a night train in Greece, I talked with two men from that day's tour. This sounds like the beginning of an Agatha Christie novel, but nothing sinister happened. At least, not on our train car. One of the men was a lawyer turned professional dancer. As the train rattled its way back to Athens, we had a lengthy chat about travel and money and family and taking risks for creative dreams.

My train friend came from a long line of lawyers, and became one mostly because he didn't want to break the family tradition. He tried it their way first, but all along the practical road, he knew that what he really wanted to do with his life was dance. After some time practicing law, he took an "impractical" flying leap toward his dancing dreams.

It may not end up being so impractical, though. In an unknown AI future, his impractical choice of dance may become the more practical option than practicing law. I say this because it doesn't seem like much of a stretch to say it'll be some time before anyone wants to watch a robot dance, while professions like law are already seeing disruptions.

You're Writing the Manual

You get to write your manual for what you're building or creating. No one else has it. And in case it looks like others have theirs all figured out, remember this: We're all just winging it. Making plans, guessing how things might go, then adjusting as needed.

The American Revolution? They were winging it.

Nike? They were winging it.

Explorers of old? Winging it.

Literally everyone creating an interesting life? Winging it.

Permission to Pivot Your Dream

We'd just sat down to dinner on the boat when Gino announced, "Josh has something to share." Considering we were at sea with limited-to-no WiFi and there had been no mention of a serious girlfriend, I assumed we weren't about to hear news of an engagement. What sort of secret news could Josh be privy to?

With the smile of someone who has interesting news to share, he got straight to the point. "We're not going to Bermuda after all. We're headed straight to New York to avoid a storm."

What?! No Bermuda? I wanted to see that place! As the disappointment wore off and I wrapped my head around our change in plans, I decided it wasn't all bad. Our early arrival and shore privileges meant we had access to Manhattan for an extra day. This meant I would actually have time to do my Christmas shopping and get packages sent off. Yay!

Sure enough, I checked the monitor in my cabin that night and there was a definite point on the line at which we had stopped heading to Bermuda and started heading more north toward New York. Or Halifax. It was hard to tell on those monitors.

In this situation, the course pivot was due to new meteorological information. As much as I love a good story and surviving a massive storm at sea would've made for a good one of those, I'm glad. A storm serious enough to reroute us would've made for bad swells which would have made for a lot of seasickness. I spent the majority of the boat journey feeling really self-satisfied that *I* didn't get seasick, and then I did and found it an experience not to be recommended.

In a similar way, there will be—*should* be—course pivots in your life. Times when you look at the current destination and say "Actually, that's not where I want to head anymore." Maybe you have just learned that it was actually never it, but you couldn't have known until you started trying for it.

Life is a continuous process of getting new information from the inside and outside and adjusting accordingly. Refusing to pivot because you're committed to seeing something through may sound really noble, but you have permission at every point of your journey to change your mind, especially based on new information and what your intuition is nudging you toward. You can't *not* get new ideas and new directions when you have grown as much as you have.

What Makes a Dreamer?

A dreamer is:

Someone with a vision of something not yet created.

Someone with a beautiful inner world that wants to get outside.

Someone who wants to explore.

Someone driven by a feeling of "I must..." and "I want...." vs "I should." We've all done lots of things motivated by "shoulds." But the kind of dreaming I'm talking about is the creating and problem-solving we'd do even if there was no one else on the planet to clap and cheer or validate us. The kind of thing we'd do even if there wasn't a financial outcome.

A dreamer is someone who knows that nagging feeling of "this isn't it."

A dreamer is a person acting or preparing to act on a possibility not yet grounded in reality—yet being the operable word.

Someone who keeps going just to see what's around the corner, and the next corner.

Someone who is curious.

Someone brave enough to try.

Someone not content with maintaining the status quo.

Someone principle-driven.

Someone willing to move and be bruised and bumped along the way.

Someone willing to fail, be lonely, be doubted, misjudged, and rejected. A lot.

Someone who is willing to believe audacious things.

Someone who sees things differently, who feels things differently.

Someone with passion and heart.

Is this you?

I suspect so. Welcome to the club, dreamer.

Unbuilding to Rebuild

If you're in a season where it feels like your decisions and actions aren't yet yielding the hoped-for results, remember this: sometimes you have to take a building down to the studs before rebuilding something you really love.

Let Yourself Just Try Stuff

You tell me your birthday is coming up and I *will* remember. This is how I ended up at a friend's birthday dinner, meeting two new friends. As one of them shared some of the things she has tried or done in her life, I expressed surprise. At first, she didn't strike me as the "try anything" sort of person, as if there's a mold all us dreamers fit neatly into.

As Debbie said, "I'll try anything." This was the view on life she'd adopted after her decades-long marriage ended and she left the nothing-going-on border town where she'd raised her family. She now feels like a butterfly, free to live life fully and finally fly.

I don't think this unassuming woman would mind any fellow traveler borrowing some of her "I'll try anything" energy, or her approach to living that includes being unafraid to try new things. Or being afraid and doing it anyway. It's the only way you see new things, find out who you are, and what you even like.

If you've still got a lengthy To Try/See/Do list, now's a great time to start shifting items to your I Tried list. Otherwise, you'll die with too many experiences untapped and what they might've shown you about yourself.

We're not talking about illicit drugs or reckless behaviors or things like "I've always wanted to try spending $100,000 on retail therapy in a SINGLE DAY." We're talking about *soul*-level things that you've always wanted to try.

You're not going to love everything you try, even when you've dreamed about it for a long time. Or you might not love it for as long as you thought you would. But how else would you have known? There are simply some things you just need to get out of your system or cross off the list so you have more attention for the things you really love. Life is too short to see everything we dream of through to completion.

And if we're intentional about what we do, we can fit a lot of trying and living in.

The decision flow chart looks like this: Is it something I've wanted to at least try? Yes? Do something about it.

Pretty simple. Pretty awesome.

Permission to Be Impractical

Try answering objections of "but it's not practical" with "you're right" and "here I go anyway."

One definition of the word practical is "likely to succeed or be effective in real circumstances."

It's often used as an admonition to think or act in a way that's perceived to be safe or risk-free.

And it's the squelcher of many a beautiful dream.

Money does need to be earned.

Bills do need to be paid.

Kids do need to be run to and fro.

Appointments need to be scheduled and kept.

Things need cleaning.

Not everything is meant to be fun.

Yes.

However.

Practicality, as it's come to be defined, is usually practiced upon others by those who've buried their own dreams in the backyard.

Or whose main aim is to live just like everyone else—vanilla.

Don't get me wrong, nothing is wrong with a contented, ordinary life. In fact, there are a lot of reasons making it just the thing to strive for. But not if you're just doing it to blend into the crowd who stopped dreaming a while ago.

Practicality was never meant to be a prison. If you've been succeeding at what you've always known and are ready to make some new dreams come true, it might be time for impracticality.

He Cast His Vote for His Dreams

Here's the story of a dreamer who left practicality for impracticality. Dan is my cousin. He's also a guy with an exceptionally fun sense of humor and very few inhibitions.

He was doing what most of us do—had a job to pay the bills, owned a home, was involved in church and service. He and his wife welcomed children into their family, and he tried to reconcile himself to this just being adult life. There were job changes and career advancements and vacations here and there. A good life. But there was something pretty big missing from Dan's life. And that was the freedom to be Creative Dan.

It seemed really impractical that he could actually do what he loved and make enough money to provide for his family doing it. What was it he really wanted to be doing? Acting, on screen, in person, whatever. Guess how many people were clapping and cheering for a family man in his early thirties to quit a stable job and support his family with acting? Yeah, not many.

Most of the advice he got was along the lines of, "You've got a great job. It's not *that* bad. You should just keep acting on the side."

He and I worked in neighboring companies and would get together periodically at lunch to talk about work and our respective dreams. Often, one or both of us was doing something about our dreams, but in corporate sameness we stayed... for years. Until the weekday lunch we met up outside our offices to get Thai food and he told me he'd put his notice in. "I'm doing it, Em." He was leaving his job to pursue full-time acting. But "it" was bigger than just that. He was casting a major vote for his dreams and choosing his creative potential and growth over safety and sameness.

Did he have everything figured out, know exactly how it would work out, have six-figures in the bank? Nope, nope, and I don't think so. But what he did have was a certainty that the timing was never going to be perfect and that he'd never know if he didn't try in earnest. He also had a wife who encouraged him to leave his job, wanting to see him happy more than she wanted continued security. It's not that he was miserable or that his job was so bad. It's just that what he wanted to do was so dang *good*.

I'm pleased to report that this happy day was several years ago and he's still living out and refining this dream. He's still involved with church and service, still happily married, still pays his bills, lives in the same house. He's just found a way to spend lots of time in the craft he loves. Also, in his work, he gets to make people laugh and light up—the world would literally be less happy if he was still talking about what he was going to do one day. If he was still wearing his collared shirt and tie and sitting in a cubicle trying to keep his dream squashed in a cardboard box, I believe he'd have some 'splainin' to do in at the end of his life as to why he never even *tried* to do something big with the creativity and drive God gave him.

Is he rich?

You want me to say "yes," I just know it. Because that's how we measure success these days.

But I actually have no idea. What I do know is that he's making it. Even if at some point he had to return to traditional employment, he's really *lived* in these past several years. What looked impractical now seems perfectly practical. And way more fun for him than his previous versions of practicality. The best news of all this is that Dan's story can be your story, too—finding something you love doing and will find a way to do (even) more of.

Listen to Your Discontent

The discontent of a principled dreamer versus a professional complainer is a ginormous gift. When we see it otherwise, we don't even give our discontent a chance to tell us important things.

We are *meant* to be dissatisfied. It's what provides fuel to even try to build and launch figurative rocket ships. If we were never dissatisfied, we would never grow. We'd remain at our first jobs and keep doing the things we were excited about twenty years ago. We'd never create new things just for the sake of creating or close chapters longing to be in our past.

It's like wearing too-small shoes. Did they used to fit you? Yes. Can you still technically cram your feet into them? Yes. Can you get used to the discomfort? Kind of. But you're going to think constantly about the poor fit as you go about the business of daily living or consider making moves forward. Ask me about the very literally too-tight shoes in which I tromped around Europe. They were a, ah, nice foil to all the exploration I was doing to expand my comfort zone by a zillion.

The feeling of having outgrown a job or an iteration of your business or dream from the past is similar. Your discontent doesn't mean that it wasn't once good or that you're ungrateful or lazy. It just means you're ready to consider something else. In fact, you might be hungry to work harder and risk more than you ever have for your next dream.

If you've been dismissing or discrediting your discontent for a while now, you may just see what priceless information you learn from it when you treat it like the gift it is.

You Can't Know What's Coming

Don't tell Stephen R. Covey, but when it comes to business, we could say that my dad did *not* "begin with the end in mind." When it comes to life, he did. He's always had big-picture focuses of his life intact: faith, family, and freedom. And basketball.

But when it came to his business, he couldn't have set out with the end in mind, because no one knew that the Internet would become a thing. And a really big thing, which allowed him to expand his business reach dramatically.

In his case, he was just aiming to provide for the family on his own terms. A windy, uncertain, and eventful road later, he'd built a successful business which he sold in his early fifties. He didn't set out to build a nationally known brand of high-end seat covers; that was tricky before the advent of the Internet. But that's what he ended up doing, by doing the very things we dreamers do: stay in the game, look for opportunities, and create and share our stuff. You never know what's coming.

Exploration Is Key

No exploration is wasted.

On my day trip to Armenia, I met Rafael. It wasn't until mid-afternoon that we got around to talking about work. How different from most social interactions, where someone's job is the first thing we inquire about.

I can't remember what sparked our conversation, perhaps just agreeing how lucky we were to be there, experiencing this pinch-me day of life. Rafael was a former corporate lawyer used to working twelve-hour days and affording a fancy lifestyle. After decades of this, he chose to walk away, recognizing that he was one of the ones living for vacation—which all too often means momentary escapes from a frantic life of getting and maintaining. In his words, he wishes he could tell people, "You guys. It—the hustle, the consumption-lifestyle, the status-chasing—is all too much."

I shared the focus of my writing work with him, and he "got it" immediately. He's lived on both sides of the spectrum: hustle-and-grind and now simplicity. And knows very clearly which he prefers. His fancy friends see some of his *lifestyle* choices as a downgrade, failing to appreciate that he intentionally chose a major *life* upgrade.

Among the many things we talked about that day, Rafael and I agreed that it really matters that you make your life what you want it to be. To know what that even is, you need to slow down, examine, and explore—figuratively and sometimes literally. You miss the life you might've created otherwise if you don't.

It Matters What Your Heart Says

Pay attention to what your heart—your soul—is trying to give you permission to do.

It might be telling you things like "you are just the one to sing" or "what you have to say is worthwhile" or "listen to this."

Your heart never tells you the things your head or other people might say: "you're not good enough" or "dreams are for kids" or "it's selfish to dream" or "it must be nice to have time to dream."

What if it's selfish *not* to dream? What if it's actually selfish to keep those talents of yours unearthed, unexplored, unshared?

Here's your hall pass to do more listening to the hollerings of your heart. And to create more space for it to tell you things.

Your heart probably isn't going to be the one telling you to get a bigger car or alter your appearance dramatically or chase status—it's going to lead you to more creativity. To being more yourself. Sometimes, it'll sing out things like "ew, not this" and other times it might be "check this out!" Talk about cool clues worth listening to from your heart and the One who made it and who wants you to really live while you're here.

Believing in You

So there I was, recovering from a hip surgery. Pain medication wasn't doing much for pain relief or sleep, and I was awake in the middle of the night, looking for something to distract myself. Inexplicably—I hadn't yet fallen in love with college football—I found myself immersed in the classic football movie *Rudy*.

This movie tells the story of a short, athletically very mediocre, working-class kid from a factory town born with a really big heart. By heart, I'm talking about passion and drive. I have no idea about the size of his anatomical heart, but his passion for football and particularly Notre Dame football was off the charts. And he had a dream bigger than he "deserved" to have.

You see, it was his lifelong dream to play football at Notre Dame, one of the best college football programs in the country. Nearly everyone in his life dismissed, poo-poo'd, or merely humored his dream. They deemed it impractical, unrealistic, and a waste of time to try. In their eyes, the sooner he ditched the dream and reconciled himself to doing what people from that town did—work at the factory—the better.

And this was tempting for Rudy. Yessiree, it sure was. But then his best friend dies in a tragic explosion at the factory, and Rudy's life is never again the same. The loss of this best friend who believed in Rudy's dreams is his wake-up call to take action toward them. He heads to Notre Dame, tells a kindly priest he wants to go to school there, and is referred to a nearby community college to get his grades up for admission at Notre Dame. He works on the grounds maintenance crew for the stadium and spends the next couple years getting rejected and demoralized. But he *finally* gets admitted to the school and attends tryouts for the football team.

There is no way this kid should make the team as he's missing some critical criteria for football: size and speed and athleticism. But he stands out for his determination and he gets the, ah, privilege, of being on the practice squad. This basically means he gets all the pummeling and none of the glory. His dream at this point, now that he's accomplished the dream of getting into Notre Dame and sort-of being on the football team, is to simply dress for a home game.

It takes a lot for this kid to stop believing in himself, but giving heart and soul to the team and having games tick by do finally bring him to a point where he's ready to quit and give up for good on that ultimate dream. Even invincible dreamers like him reach breaking points.

At this critical juncture a mentor, Fortune—a dreamer who quit on his own dream—says strongly worded things to Rudy, reminding him of how far he's come, how much he's overcome, and HOW DARE YOU QUIT NOW? Rudy digs deep for the umpteenth time and, spoiler alert, finally gets the chance to dress for a game. Oh happy day. I'll keep any remaining details quiet in case you want to watch it for the first time, but I must say, it's quite the movie. Enough for me to watch it TWICE in that one hippy night. And cry both times, and every time I've watched it since.

I'm a sucker for redemption stories like these.

The general plot of these true stories go something like this—and tell me if this doesn't just resonate big with you and your dreams:

Main character has a thing he loves doing.

He does or wants to do the thing in his younger years but then there's a BAD THING—an injury or family upheaval or other tragic thing—that makes it seem impossible.

He tries to get back to it, but it just doesn't seem meant to be.

He lives beneath his potential for a long, lame time, and tries hard to forget about the dream or his audacity to ever have it in the first place.

Then, one day, something sparks his "impractical" dream back to life. We then see him do things like pushing tires, throwing sports balls in the headlights, getting out of bed in the wee hours of the morning to exercise. Basically, he starts believing in himself in a new way, and doing things about it. And, wouldn't you know, it's about this time that he gets a break.

The big one.

But the big break is not what gave him permission to believe in his dream again.

He was doing that for himself.

And so can you, as long as you're doing something about those dreams of yours.

The Wonder of Creating Badly

If you picked up a book called *Dear Fellow Dreamer* you've got stuff to create. Loads of it.

You were born to actively create, not passively consume. The bad news is that very few of us intrinsically know how to do the former; the latter comes very easy.

If you don't even know what exactly you want to create, take heart. The clarity is coming. Or you'll find it. As long as you don't do nothing, give up, spin in busy work, over-consume self-help and digital courses, make excuses for why it can never be different, or live in chaos and squalor. I don't know that many people live in actual squalor, but it's too good of a word to pass up, regardless of what my editor says.

In order to create anything worthwhile, you've got to create badly at first, and perhaps for a very long time. So here's the explicit permission to prioritize your creativity, and keep prioritizing it regardless of the perceived outcomes.

Official sanction is hereby granted to create loads of hooey and a perfect *mountain* of failed creative ideas and attempted dreams. The alternative is listening to the siren song of "getting ready to be creative" or stalled in lame consumption mode. And it just has never been possible to consume your way to your dreams.

The Best is Not Behind You

As alluded to in the introduction, I spent a couple post-corporate years traveling. When you travel off the beaten path, you meet gobs of new friends. And you connect differently with people from your past who are doing similar things. You "get" each other in a way that people safe at home may not.

One such friend I reconnected with was a friend from high school who shared, "When I was younger, it helped a lot to know that I still had a lot of life left and a lot more to accomplish. At this age, I don't feel old, but I also don't feel that sense of still being on the way up." This friend was definitively not talking about getting more stuff or having a fancy schmancy house or professional accolades. What he wanted is what all dreamers want, and that's a sense of purpose and satisfaction that only comes from doing hard things to get that priceless "I did it" feeling.

Maybe you can relate to it feeling too late for you. Or like your opportunities to do some of the things that excite you are officially expired or recalled like the breakfast cereal I tried to buy months back. I was taken aback when the cashier, AJ, told me "I can't sell you that"—like I'd tried to buy contraband instead of tame Quaker Oat Squares.

You're not too old to still do cool things. We're talking about cool things as defined by you, not things you think will earn you "cool" status to anyone else.

Picture a stage musical. The stage is crowded with all the singing and dancing people. You're engrossed in the menagerie of it all—the costumes, the effects, the music. And all of a sudden the main character emerges from that happily chaotic crowd, where they'd been subtly blending in until their big moment.

This is what it looks like for those who decide that their best creations and contributions are still ahead, and who get serious about bringing any one of their ideas to life. It's like they emerge from the background of a stage scene to reveal themselves as the main character of their life. And if this sounds selfish, is it more honorable to spend your time blending in and deferring to others? If you believe in God like I do, you might also believe that He didn't put us here to be just like everyone else, or to spend all our time trying to blend in.

Am I selling you on the idea that it might not be too late for you? Good. I'm sold myself. But just in case you've been needing explicit permission to believe a good measure of the best is still ahead of you, here's your hall pass. Permission granted to still be on the way up to exciting things, to take up something completely new—whether you're twenty-nine or forty-five or fifty-seven or seventy-six. To believe that you haven't even scratched the surface on discovering and sharing your talents and interests, to take center stage of your own life, to believe that as good as your life has been and is, the best is still yet to be.

Assume Permission

You guys. Remember CDs and the padded cases full of them? The bulky stereo in your home with a stack of CDs in plastic cases near it? In the early 2000s, I got all kinds of jazzed about the fact my Mitsubishi Galant had a CD changer conveniently located in the trunk of the car. This made it so I could—get this—put six CDs in it and choose *from the front* which CD I wanted to listen to. We'd really reached the pinnacle of technological advancement and convenience.

Except then there were mp3s and iPods, and now we have streaming services where we have access to all the music in the world. Not hyperbole. And innovation in musical access is just one small part of life. Expanding this to creative domains and appreciate this: it's literally never been easier to create whatever you want. It's *almost like* the Universe has conspired for our good to provide all the things we need to do the things we say we want to do.

Write a book? Well, Amazon KDP—Kindle Direct Publishing—and companies like them have made getting a book out in to the world infinitely easier than forty years ago when you had to either find a publisher, be found by them, or buy thousands of copies of your own book to sell out of the trunk of your car.

Start a business? Okay, great news. You can do your own graphic design using Canva. Print-on-demand companies will create your designed products and ship directly to your customers. There are amazing course hosting platforms, email management systems, and web platforms that, sure, take some effort to learn or money to have someone to do the thing for you, but the bar has never been lower. Add to this that AI makes possible even wild ideas you might've ruled out before.

Basically, it's literally never been less expensive or more accessible for us to make things, to try things, to learn things. If you wait for explicit, external permission that your dream is good and worthwhile and that it's going to work, you could be waiting a very long time. Someone else is just going to assume permission and do it. And you can start doing that with the best of them.

Permission to Keep Trying

If you've been trying for some time now to do something wonderful, take heart. Most people don't ever do the things you've already done, or entertain the hopes you do for a meaningful life.

No more beating yourself up for where you are or are not. You've been learning exactly what you need to know and being refined for your best work. If it's not happening on your timeline, it doesn't mean anything is going wrong. There's no failure in buying yourself and your dream more time.

Very few remarkable things happen overnight—it's why we typically get long lives and a lot of persistence. No book worth reading was written in a week. Months and years and fortunes are spent creating most of the projects we ever come to know about.

Summiting Everest is notable because it's not exactly a small hill which can easily be conquered. The story of Earnest Shackleton's exploration party is captivating precisely *because* it was really hard and really long and really uncertain. They somehow found the proverbial joy in the journey to their goal of, oh, not dying. We humans tend to love the success stories that were preceded by long chapters of adventure and angst and things not working out. We like them less when we're living them, which is why it matters so much that you give yourself permission to be gentle with your road, and keep trying.

You're where you need to be, and you're becoming exactly who you need to be for your funnest and best work.

You Don't Have to Know How It Turns Out

It—life and what you're making of it—wouldn't be an adventure at all if you knew exactly how it was all going to work out.

Doing What's Good for You

Often what is good for you is to do the brave thing and keep creating, to press on and keep trying to move your dream forward.

But sometimes, what's good for you and your dream might be to pivot, pause or withdraw to a position of safety, and replenish your stores or energy. As the aphorism goes: "The wisest generals know when to retreat." Retreating doesn't mean ceding the war. You may just need to get some perspective, catch your breath, and come at it again from another angle instead of trying the same ol' thing. Things have a way of working out for people with grit, but the timeline for results is God's department.

For entrepreneurs, doing what's good for you may mean returning to work that isn't your dream to get more runway for your dreams. There may also be things you need or want to learn about that you can get paid to learn. Building your dreams can be lonely, draining business even if incredibly worthwhile. You may actually *want* to help build someone else's dream for a season in exchange for one of those paycheck things. But there can be drama around this since people sometimes make it mean way more than it does: "That's too bad YOUR DREAM didn't work out and you had to return to a JOB."

Who said the dream isn't still alive and well?

Caleb is a fellow dreamer and one I guarantee you'd love sitting next to on any bus. We worked at the same company several years ago and didn't know the other was entrepreneurial until he left first to go out on his own. The day I saw that he had, I messaged him on LinkedIn, with some of that "You left! What's it like out there on your own?" energy.

When I left corporate a few months after him, he was one of the first people I reached out to. He's a rare person—generous, humble, principled, smart—and was excited for my leap. Over the years, we've stayed in touch about business and life here and there. Caleb's personal life shifted in exciting ways over the recent years, and I saw on LinkedIn that his title had changed. It appeared he had taken a professional job, something which surprised me as he seemed the consummate entrepreneur. But here's the thing: he still *is* the consummate entrepreneur. He still has his own aims and plans and businesses. He's just doing what all dreamers do: finding ways to support himself and his family while refining his vision and plans for his own stuff.

As we talked about his current job, it was clear that he's very much not *owned* by any opportunity he takes. Knowing him, he's a great employee, but as he put it, "They're renting me, not buying me."

My own experiences of leaving jobs multiple times for seasons of exploration have been critical to my personal growth. And when I've returned to jobs when that was good for me, it's been with an increased skillset, a clearer view of what kind of life I'm creating, and appreciation for a paycheck to temporarily fund my life while I work on the next phase of my dreams.

Even old-time explorers bravely navigating new territory and doing hard things like living on lousy crackers and bad jerky, finding ways over or around mountains, and recovering yet again from dysentery and scurvy needed reprieves. They visited forts to restock, to rest up, to repair their tents, to catch their breath, to swap stories. And not because they were no longer explorers, but because it was what was good for them in between legs of the adventure.

Listen to what you need, do what's good for you, and don't make it mean anything more than it does—which is not a thing.

Move On

Sometimes it's simply time to move on. To close a chapter. To leave some stuff behind and start something fresh. No explanation or justification necessary.

Permission to Be Ordinary

You might actually love your work and life right now, but feel like you *should be* doing more important things. I have *no idea* why you'd feel this way. I mean, we are only swimming in Instagram Reels and TikTok videos of people doing "important" things or living "important" lives. It can seem like everyone and their kid and their dog is winning awards, being picked first for figurative teams, making fancy professional lists, going fabulous places, hitting certain subscriber milestones. The list goes on and on and is happening basically everywhere on the Internet where most of us spend lots of time.

We all like to share our wins, with some people doing so much more than others, and besides some of it feeling braggartly, there's perhaps nothing intrinsically wrong with doing so. Some of it is an essential part of owning a business or promoting creative work and helping your stuff find the people you made it for. That said, living for the purpose of making fancy lists or getting social media likes can literally never satisfy our thirst for meaningful living, and it sure ruins "ordinary" happy living.

Dreams and longings were never given to us for external approval or to get us "important" points. We have them to keep us from languishing on figurative or literal couches or in stale cubicles or office chairs we've figuratively outgrown. If you actually love the "ordinary" life you're creating right now and know you're growing and developing like God wants for you, revel in that. You get all the *actually* important points.

"Explore the Space"

There's a *Saturday Night Live* skit where Will Farrell is the cowbell player in a band. Naturally. The director likes what they're doing, but really wants "MORE COWBELL." He encourages Will Farrell to "really explore the space."

Now, you're no cowbell player, or, if you actually are, I want to know you. You nonetheless might need to explore the space more. And in this case, the space is you and your interests and *life in general*. You are who you are for a reason, and you were never meant to dismiss your talents, passions, and dreams, or limit yourself to what you currently know and like.

The band is in session and here's your authorization to really get out there, be you, and *play*. May I recommend that you really explore the space and whack that figurative cowbell with everything you've got.

You Have Lots of Chances

Ralph Waldo already made an appearance earlier in the book, but there's one other gem from "Self-Reliance" you've just got to know about.

In it, Ralph contrasts city boys who lose heart after a single failed enterprise to the "sturdy lad from New Hampshire or Vermont." Apparently those were the only states producing sturdy lads back then. About these sturdy lads, he said, "[They who] tried all the professions, who *teams it, farms it, peddles*, keeps a school, preaches, edits a newspaper, goes to Congress, buys a township, and so forth in successive years, and always, like a cat, falls on his feet." According to Ralph, this lad "is worth a hundred of these city dolls. He walks abreast with his days, and feels no shame in not 'studying a profession,' for he does not postpone his life, but lives already. He has not one chance but a hundred chances."[11]

Even if you're not from New Hampshire or Vermont, if you're willing to venture and aren't a city doll, you don't just get one chance. You get one hundred chances, maybe more. *If* you approach life willing to try, that is. One hundred chances are what you give yourself when you give yourself permission to try lots of things. If I could go back to College Emily, I would give her a serious pep talk about how she would get a multitude of chances in life to get things "right," whatever that even means.

Here's the preemptive permission to not make our decisions so loaded, and to move forward on any idea that feels at least pretty good, with the sure knowledge that you will have lots of chances to get it (life) right. If you let yourself practice and create and try a lot of things, you'll get lots of chances to stick the landings on things that really matter. Very few decisions in our lives are permanent and that, my dreamer friends, is very good news.

3

FREQUENTLY ASKED QUESTIONS

We're all familiar with Frequently Asked Questions. Right? If you're not, I'm sorry but you missed some critical life exposure somewhere along the way and I have serious concerns about your ability to navigate in the world. Google "FAQs" if you must, but the rest of us are going to continue on.

This section of the book came out of a conversation with a fellow traveler considering making a big leap into the unknown. We'd talked for forty-five minutes before he asked the question he really wanted to ask: "What do you do about self-doubt?"

It's good and bad news that dreaming big and taking action is a situation highly customized to each person brave enough to try. But we dreamers have things in common, including the "embarrassing" questions we rarely utter out loud. Why we feel like we should have it together and have our next steps all figured out, I do not know. The reality is that literally anyone doing anything worthwhile that they haven't done before, and which may not have been done by anyone, more often than not is going to be thinking, "I have literally no clue what I'm doing right now."

Unlike a company or an entrepreneur selling a product or service, I can't give you assurances of success and there's no refund policy for taking the risks you're contemplating. There are no magic-bullet answers or neat and tidy steps to reaching any of your dreams. But it's reassuring to know you are not the only one asking these sorts of questions. I've asked them, and anyone venturing or thinking about venturing has them, too. Pretend, if you like, that we are around a campfire, late at night, talking about what really matters, and these questions finally come up. These are the vulnerable questions every dreamer worth their salt will ask—and need to answer—multiple times on the worthwhile road. I'll go first with my answers, but make note of your own since the way you answer these questions in thought and action will shape your dreams.

Am I Being Irresponsible or Brave?

The good news is that only you can know the answer to this question. That's also the bad news. If every dreamer had a guaranteed outcome of success, our airspace would be chock full of intrepid explorers leaping right and left. "There's another one leaving their stable job!" Or "Would you look at that? She's opening her own art studio!" Or "Now he's writing a YA novel? Cool!" Or "I didn't know he always wanted to run for office!" Or "She bought a *castle*?!"

There are "responsible" people who will stamp every leap that doesn't work out within the first five minutes with the label "IRRESPONSIBLE." Does that make it *actually* irresponsible? No. They've not been part of the hoping and dreaming and planning and feeling stuck and the deep knowing that you're being called to step into The Unknown.

Those with very low risk-tolerances will think anything with less than 100% chance of success is foolhardy. And sometimes their thinking can creep into ours. Try these questions as you size up your possible brave leap or your next steps on the path you're already walking.

Do you have at least some of your ducks in a row?

Do you have at least some idea of what you think is possible with this venture?

Have you come to trust yourself with time and money?

Do you have a plan for returning to safety if need be?

Have you tried to improve things within your safe situation to avoid a premature exit?

Do you have *some* safety net?

Are you just burying your head in the sand and ignoring reality?

What's at stake if you don't make your leap?

Whose definitions of "irresponsible" and "brave" are informing yours?

What else will help *you* determine whether you're being irre-sponsible or brave?

What About When It's "Not Working Out?"

First of all, who says it's not working out? Is it *really* not working out, or just not working out *yet*?

"Working out" is a pretty arbitrary measuring stick anyway, and often more of a feeling than a provable reality.

And even when things actually don't "work out," it's usually because you've reached the end of a chapter so you can write the next one or entertain the one headed your way thanks to a chapter you wrote ages ago.

It's natural to hope that taking the leap will instantly unveil all your answers, that everything works out swimmingly and faster than expected. When it doesn't work out immediately, you might be asking if it was or if it is still "worth it." You get to answer that question for yourself, probably over and over.

Personally, I'd say a resounding "Heck yes!" because it's not over. You're not over. You're still just scraping the surface of your potential. Also, what if the thing you think fell flat is actually THE THING that eventually gets your work dis-covered? Just because it didn't fly fast, doesn't mean it's not going to fly, and fly far.

Jimmy Stewart, of *It's A Wonderful Life* fame, was already a fancy actor before he opted to deploy for active combat in World War II. Against the strong recommendations of military top brass, he also chose to lead flying bombing missions over enemy territory. They wanted a famous actor to stay safe, but he wanted to serve his country in this way.

The experiences he had purportedly aged him far beyond his thirty-seven years. He'd been a dashing and sought-after star before the war, and came home depressed, gaunt, and mentally shot. A changed man, Stewart received no acting offers until Frank Kafka talked him into playing George Bailey in *It's A Wonderful Life*. He almost declined the role because it felt too heavy for his first film post-war. But the heaviness of his war experiences were what made him such a success in the role of a good man who, in his desperation over financial troubles, considers ending his life. Stewart's biographer Robert Matzen said about his acting in the film, "I don't think he had that kind of capacity before the war."[12]

What's also worth talking about is the fact that this now-classic film was a "box-office *flop*" when it came out in 1946.[13] And the story on which it was based—a short story by Philip Van Doran Stern called *The Greatest Gift*—initially also appeared to be a flop. "Unable at first to find a publisher...Stern ultimately published the story in a small pamphlet and sent it out as his 1943 Christmas card. One of those 200 cards found its way into the hands of Frank Capra, who shared it with Jimmy Stewart."[14]

You never know how things will sort out for dreamers who stay in the game—even, or especially, when they don't know how things are working out.

How Do I Handle Other People's "Easy" Success?

Unless you are Mother Theresa or Ghandi or Luna Lovegood from the *Harry Potter* book series, you can't help but see others winning with seemingly much less effort than you've been putting in, and experience some really exciting feelings like jealousy and envy.

Your options for handling this terrific experience include the following:

1. Wonder what you're doing wrong and what they're doing right, and assume that you're just not meant for success like some people no matter how hard you try. This is the approach I, from experience, recommend least. In fact, I give it zero stars.

2. Call your best business friend and talk about HOW VERY HAPPY you are for the overnight success of the ones whose brand-new product or offering took off within days or weeks. It's amazing how much it can help to find humor in your human foibles. And also to appreciate that these dreamers will have their own opportunities for growth and reflection and may, at some point, end up learning from your more windy road.

3. Appreciate that the "times and seasons" talked about Ecclesiastes are very real. And that your thing's time simply has not come. The timing and success of others has absolutely nothing to do with yours.

The critical thing to learn and remember is that we each, for real, have our own lanes. This does not mean you change nothing about the way you are doing things or don't try to learn from the success of others. You focus on your race, celebrate those of others, and work through the feelings of jealousy and envy which—let's just be honest—are going to arise. Part of creating a life of your own is learning to love exactly what *you've* received, timing and all.

What If I Fail Spectacularly and Publicly?

Well, what if you do? It's worth answering that question for yourself.

About failing publicly, I'll say that you'll waste loads of effort trying to "guess it right" or perfect your thing safely hidden from the public eye.

I can't think of very many ventures or products or creative works that weren't preceded by at least *some* public preparation and effort. Sometimes they succeeded right out of the gate. Some of them appeared to crash and burn. Some adventurer's steps toward what finally worked for them appeared to be failures. Until the day one of their things succeeded, and the rest got grandfathered in and wildly celebrated.

There is literally no way to know what's going to work. Possible public failure is the price of admission to play the game of A Life Worth Living.

Should I Just Play It Safe Until _____?

Okay. This might be the most important conversation we have. This question—should I just play it safe until I know what the future looks like?—becomes even more relevant when we're facing an AI future of profound uncertainty. Yes, *profound*. Some people say we could lose gobs of jobs within a handful of years. Others say it could take longer, like a whopping decade. Some experts want to pause AI for decades while we build up guardrails that prevent it from displacing humans, but that seems highly improbable. Literally no one knows what the future holds, what economies will be like, or what creative fields may look like. But that's been true even before AI.

Here's what I know: There will never be a perfect time to do any one of your things. There will only be the time that feels right for you. And what appears foolhardy to others may end up serving you in profound ways in the future.

If you're waiting for all global unrest to resolve, for the economy to be stable with a guaranteed future, for peace between elections, for perfect health and energy, and on and on, you're going to grow old waiting. Humanity, in the future, may end up really placing a very high value on authentic human (not AI) creativity, paying a premium for the very thing you're just waiting to create or do. The job that feels so stable right now may be keeping you from employing your talents in ways that could be the most worthwhile thing for you in the future.

There's never been a better time to do your thing than the time you get the inspired pushes to do it. You don't know where it will lead and, most importantly, how it might change everything about your life or perspective on it all.

There's a memorable story in *The 4-Hour Workweek* by Tim Ferriss, where he talks about this very thing. He wrote the following about a man named Jean-Marc Hachey:

"Sometimes timing is perfect...Other times, the timing could be better." And then goes on to describe how the timing of Hachey's volunteer experience could've been better, "from a more selfish survival standpoint...The national menu had changed and they were out of luxuries like bread and water. He would be surviving for four months on a slushlike concoction of corn meal and spinach."

Sound pretty bad? Well, once he got used to it, Jean-Marc ended up being totally fine with the daily menu and with the experience overall. It profoundly reshaped the rest of his life. He lives comfortably now, but knows he could lose it all and be fine—he lived with nothing before and knows he could be perfectly content with a little gruel and people he cares about.[15]

A person sure doesn't get these kinds of stories if they hide in a cave, waiting for things to be safer before venturing. For dreamers, it's tremendously empowering to know that it's never going to be completely safe to do your thing or try to make a life of your own. You're going to be fine, you're going to adjust and pivot and innovate, and you're going to really live. No matter what happens or doesn't happen, you're going to get way better stories than you'll get by waiting.

What If I Don't Like It?

I doubt I'm the only dreamer to have hesitated before fully committing, out of fear that I may not even like doing the thing I'm considering doing. Because this is a book about dreams and creativity, you get to like what you try. The thing is, though, a lot of times we don't know what we're going to like. With at least occasional self-doubt, human moods, and creative resistance, we can be lousy judges of what we might like and what we won't. There really is only one way to find out whether you'll like something or not, and it's to try it.

And to ask often and all along the way, "Do others need this from me?" And "How will this help other people?" Questions like these magically dissipate nearly every bad mood or inclination to "not feel like doing the thing." Ask questions like these and your gaze is lifted from stagnant navel watching and back into the world of possibilities.

There's a book, *Thinking in Bets,* by Annie Duke. She's a former professional poker player turned consultant, author, and speaker. For some reason, "professional poker player" never came up in conversations about my future with my high school guidance counselor. Did I even *have* a high school guidance counselor? If so, I don't know if we actually spoke. And if we did, I don't think there was much guidance being solicited or given. I digress.

Duke's book, by even title alone, is quite the pep talk. When you're facing a decision, whether it be an initial step or a pivot, making a solid bet is the best you can do. And if you bet wrong, remember that so do lots of others, and you get to bet on something else.

What Do I Tell People Who Think I'm Crazy?

You don't tell them much, that's what. But because it's awkward to walk away in silence from these conversations where others want you to explain yourself or your dream to them, here are some potential lines to use.

"I'm working on some projects I'm excited about."

"I'm not talking too much about it these days, but appreciate your support!"

"It may not be your thing, but I'm really excited about it."

The key is to stay vague, and out of the emotional arena where you're trying to get buy-in on your idea from someone who's probably totally lovely, but who's not capable of believing in your dreams—until you make them happen.

What If My People Don't Approve?

This may sound silly, but hear me out. No matter how old you are or how independent and self-assured you've become, there's a part of all of us who just wants to hear our parents and our people gush over us and our endeavors like they do about your high school friend who's now wildly successful.

But your people—no matter how you love and admire and respect each other—may not "get" what it is you're hoping to do. If you're lucky, they'll understand when they see it, and when it makes sense in a way they can explain it to their friends and peers. They can love you and not remotely understand your dream—yet. They just can't see it like you can or like you're trying to.

If you don't get much buy-in from your people, the biggest favor you can do for yourself and your relationships with them, is to stop trying to make them understand. Let them not "get" it and perhaps never express that they're inordinately proud of you. And know you have plenty of dreamer company in this. Steve Martin, for example, talks candidly about his father's critical take on his work in his book, *Born Standing Up.* His father's withheld praise and outright criticism stung, but Steve can view it now with compassion and understanding.

It helps to know that some of these people we love are, like Steve Martin's father, sitting on their own graveyard of buried dreams. It's understandably complicated that they may never celebrate your dreams or accomplishments like you wish for. The sooner you stop trying to earn their approval, the more you will be free to create, to love them without strings, and to make *yourself* proud for all your efforts along the way.

It further helps to assume that deep down—even if it's *really* down there—they are positively *gushing* with praise for you, the bravest dreamer they know.

What About Self-Doubt?

Ah yes, beloved self-doubt. As mentioned in the introduction of this section, several weeks ago I received a call from someone I know. He wanted to tell me about the flying leap he was considering taking—leaving his stable job, going into business for himself, taking a chance on himself. There are certain subject matters for which I stayed up well past my bedtime to talk on the phone, and this tops the charts.

I will always make time to talk with any person daring enough to believe in their abilities and consider that there could be more to their life than just collecting a paycheck and hoping they're not in the next round of layoffs. And, in his case, that they don't quadruple his responsibilities without additional compensation—again. All of a sudden, his stable job doesn't look so stable.

The caller knew that I'd be excited for him. And he also knew that, because I've not had my own meteoric rise (yet) but still find what I am doing immensely worthwhile, he could be more vulnerable with me than with some others. Somewhere in the middle of our call, he brought it up: "So...I can get mired in my head and in self-doubt. What do you do about that?"

Now *that's* a question.

I know this self-doubt thing of which he speaks. It's something that all non-egomaniac creators and dreamers bent on growth over comfort know. Sometimes in spades. Despite what some digital influencers say, there's no neat and tidy seven-step digital course that actually works for mastering self-doubt. Of course, there are things that help lessen or quiet it; I'm not suggesting you just throw up your hands in surrender to its presence.

Here's what I've learned you do about self-doubt: You face it. You may never permanently fix it, but it also may not be something to be fixed. You get out of bed each morning. You prove your self-doubt wrong by doing the things it tried to keep you from doing. You treat yourself with compassion. When your self-doubt is extra loud, you set it up on the couch with a show and some snacks while you go be a grown-up who's working on something exciting. You recognize that some things are just so worth doing, even if self-doubt insists on coming along for the ride.

I said, "if"? I mean, "when," since self-doubt *always* tags along if you're doing something interesting or stretching. It just doesn't get to drive the bus, not anymore at least.

What About Rejection?

If you haven't already started accumulating your long list of rejections and failures, it's not too late. For a dreamer bent on creating a life of their own, rejection will take many fun forms—times when it feels like nothing is happening, outright no's, people dismissing or misunderstanding what it is you're doing. Rejection is a feature in an interesting life, not a bug.

People, however, love to talk about their successes, wins, and acceptance. The most interesting people, though, also talk about their "failures" and their rejections, of which there will be many.

You'll like this from Davis Smith, the founder of Cotopaxi, a brand I adore for their neon colors. In a LinkedIn post which could've been called an "ode to rejection," he shared: "I keep a list of every VC I have ever pitched. The list comprises over 800 investors. When raising money for Cotopaxi, I was rejected hundreds and hundreds of times. It never changed my belief that the brand needed to exist."[16]

Remember this when you're tempted to hold your rejections against yourself or your dreams:

1. You literally cannot get successes without them.

2. Only intrepid souls get them.

3. They're the most important part of the whole thing.

How Long Do I Try?

Five months. That's how long you try. I'm entirely kidding. There is no "right" or universal answer to this question. There's only the answer you work out between yourself and God.

So much has to do with your individual personality, your personal tolerance for risk, the circumstances of your life, how much you have in savings, what your endeavor actually is, what feelings you're getting from God regarding your next steps.

For some of your dreams, you might just need to take a few steps in their general direction to realize, "Cool, not what I actually thought, can cross it off my list." Others may hold your deep interest and commitment for years.

Some dreams can temporarily return to a holding shelf if need be. Others you may have put on the shelf only to discover later that their time has finally come. Case in point: Our girl L.M. Montgomery wrote the classic series *Anne of Green Gables,* only to have it rejected by several publishers. A few years later, she rediscovered it, tried again, and it became an almost instant success when it was published a year later. Go figure.

4

TRAIL MARKERS

S o, you know how explorers of old would leave signs and clues for each other that they were on the right track? You know, by ripping off pieces off their itchy woolen shirts and hanging them on branches. Or they'd give recommendations to explorers coming after them, "So, what you're going to want to do is, when you see the tree that looks like an ostrich's neck, hang a left and go another seventeen canoe lengths and you'll find the coziest cave..."

Or, when they'd meet up at forts or bump into each other on the open seas, they'd get advice from someone who'd gone ahead, and swap stories with others doing the brave things. I have no idea how much this actually happened, and they probably didn't rip up their one precious shirt. Also, this isn't a history book.

But I do know that esteemed leaders like George Washington studied maps of past military campaigns and accounts from explorers and military heroes throughout his life. That study was part of what prepared him to be the remarkable leader we remember. I am definitely not in the same league as George

Washington, or explorers like Jim Bridger or Ernest Shackleton. On the Lewis and Clark expedition, I would've been left beside the trail *long* before they ever made it to my home state of Montana.

For our purposes, though, I don't need to be an explorer of old to have done *a lot* of exploring of present-day uncertainty. To non-adventurers of our time, a lot of it doesn't make sense. To dreamers, though, it will. I can thus share with you the many things I've learned the hard way to make your own exploring a little bit easier. You are wildly correct that there's no easy path to anywhere worthwhile, but you maybe don't need to learn all my things the same hard way.

This section of this book is meant to be returned to whenever you need a lesson learned, practical guidance, or strategies to try—from a dreamer a few adventures and risks ahead of you on this party of living wide-awake.

Quick Fixes to Stuck

When you're feeling stuck in your head or in your life, try one or multiple of these:

Clean something, anything.

Clean up your budget.

Brush your teeth.

Brush your hair.

Brush your pet.

Send a nice text to someone.

Make your bed.

Tidy your room.

Tidy your office.

Tidy your desk.

Listen to a favorite *happy* song.

Tackle one item from your to-do stack.

Write down the pesky negative thoughts rattling around in the ol' tin can upstairs.

Wash dishes.

Write down five things you're grateful for right now.

Walk around the block.

Go get the mail.

Run a quick errand.

Vacuum something.

Shower.

Listen to even a few minutes of a podcast or inspirational book.

Pray.

Water the bonsai tree you're trying desperately to keep alive.

Make yourself smile.

Watch something funny.

Write down three nice things about yourself.

Growing a Dream

Here are a few things this non-green thumb garden appreciator knows about growing a dream.

Thinking + talking about it = Shade.

Taking action = Sun.

Managing your attention = Watering.

Simplifying = Weeding so the good can grow.

Share Carefully

Be careful whose advice you take or with whom you share your dreams.

Other people are not meant to understand your dream at the outset. Some will, but most won't. They'll get it one day and you can include them at that point.

Until then, you risk, if you share too widely, getting your dream dismissed or downgraded or deflated or judged. And that's not good.

Enthusiasm Is Gold

Doing what you're doing with enthusiasm is the ultimate act of venturing, of belief in yourself and your idea.

Whatever you're doing, try doing it with some gusto.

Find Fellow Travelers

It can get a bit lonely out here on the trail. I'm of course referring to the figurative trail every principled dreamer knows and is willing to hike. And it's where you find all the adventure and growth and new discoveries and kindred spirits. I, for one, have come to appreciate the examples of regular people who are willing to forgo titles, security, explanations, and, in the words of a Substack friend, "tidy plans," in order to discover new possibilities and do something about their potential.

There's absolutely nothing tidy about taking flying leaps and believing in yourself and your dream enough to take action. But from where the famous sit in their fancy podcast studios, hosting other mega-millionaires and talking about their early days, we sometimes get their overly-peppy or over-simplified versions of "Gosh, it was hard, but it was worth it. You can do it, too!"

Don't get me wrong. There are certainly things to learn from the stories of many successful people, especially the ones who genuinely seem to remember where they started and whose famous life doesn't actually appear to be quite miserable. There's just some invaluable support and inspiration we can get from those traveling alongside or a few miles ahead of us. There's a collegial "Come on you guys, we can do it!" feeling to these stories.

Too often though, these stories stay quiet until the externally validated major success occurs. At that point, the world at large is like "Okay, *now* your story is worthwhile." I'm here to say that the story you're writing as you really put your back into living is worthwhile *the whole way through*. Whether you ever get that societal stamp of approval or not. Whether it ever "works out" or not. The figurative writing of that story will be much less lonely if and as you find fellow dreamers bent on also creating a substantial life of their own.

Convincing Yourself

The most important person you need to convince of the worth-whileness of your work and endeavor is *yourself*.

Why is your idea or your creative work fabulous?

Why do people need it, and uniquely from you?

What do *you* love about your work?

Is there something you would rather be doing instead? I doubt it.

Self-doubting Thoughts

If you've got big plans as I know you do, your thoughts are either going to help you big, or hinder you big. The default thoughts we all think have a marvelous wash of squashing ambition and determination.

One thought that will only get you as far as the nearest 7-Eleven convenience store to buy an hours-old hot dog is this one: "There's already too much of my thing in the world."

Another is that it will be self-aggrandizing to put your stuff out there.

Or that there's really nothing special about your perspective.

Or that you are just "small stuff."

Or that you need to drop twenty pounds before you'll feel confident enough to do your thing.

How glad we all are that when other dreamers thought these hindering thoughts, they didn't entertain them long or permanently enough to stop them from what ended up being their best work.

Planting vs Harvesting Seasons

Don't compare your planting season to the harvest season of another.

Another Chance to Have a Great Day

Every day is another chance to make it a great day.

And the ones that are not so great are a chance to keep going anyway, try to turn them around, and remember that even the crummiest days will end.

You get another chance at a great day tomorrow.

Humility = Your Secret Weapon

Humility is your secret weapon.

I like to get my best advice from rappers with hyphenated names. And to that end, Ice-T once shared memorable life advice. "A player never turns down a job." My source on this is a guy I met on a dating app named Jeff, so we know it's credible. Jeff heard it somewhere once and it stuck with him as great life advice. And now it's stuck with me.

Said Jeff is a man of many creative talents and gets many fancy jobs in film and photography production, but he's also not too good for small jobs that some peers might consider beneath them. He charges the same daily rate regardless of the job, so why should it matter to him if he's doing fancy stuff or grunt stuff?

This attitude has kept him happily self-employed and building his dreams for years, while I'm sure confusing all kinds of people who wonder what exactly he does for a living. Sometimes he's on sets, other times he's driving a moving truck with props across state lines. Can't you just hear the question? "But what do you *do*?"

He's staying in the game and working his craft, with no need for accolades or status, that's what he's doing.

Reverse Engineer Your Dreams

Sometimes it's easier to know what is *wrong* than it is to know at the outset what is *right*. Learning the former can lead you to the latter.

If you're having trouble articulating your dreams or the next iteration of them, try reverse engineering your way to them by paying attention to what you *don't* want or don't want anymore. How you *don't* want to spend your days, the types of work you *don't* want to do, the types of clients you *don't* want, the projects that *don't* light you up. What you *don't* want to write or paint or dance or create anymore. You're not being difficult. No one says you have to try and enjoy everything and do it forever, now did they?

We're not talking about the bits and pieces that bug you a little bit here and there. We're talking about the stuff that just doesn't work for you long-term or anymore. We all have our list of such things, especially we dreamers for whom "status quo forever" sounds like the pits.

Grow the Comfort Zone

Picture your comfort zone as if it correlates to the length of a string on a kite. A shorter string doesn't let you cover much ground. With a long string, though, you can travel to some pretty epic places. Every brave thought you entertain and every brave thing you do expands the comfort zone and puts another inch on the ol' kite string.

Stop Pushing Uphill

I'll never forget his unexpected comment: "You're really strong."

We humans remember most compliments, but this one from a lanky college kid gets remembered mostly because it was wildly unearned.

On a dark winter night, I was driving down a mountain canyon when I saw a car just off the side of the road. A small group of people stood near it, and I thought they might need my headlights since it looked as though they were looking for something. But it turns out this group of college kids was stuck in the deeper-than-it-appeared snow, had been for some time, and were trying to push their way out.

There was a young woman in the driver's seat, and her three guy friends were pushing with all their might. From the front. *Up*hill. That was Problem One. Problem Two was that the driver had the wheel cranked all the way toward the road.

I bet you can see why they weren't getting unstuck.

I offered to join with them in their current attempts. Skeptical that I was going to make much of a difference, they nonetheless agreed, and we pushed a few times from the front making—shockingly—no headway.

At this point, I suggested we tweak a few things. I asked the girlfriend to straighten out the wheels until we got momentum, at which point she would steer toward the road. Then I asked the guys to help me push from *behind* the car. Downhill, you know, and employing the ol' "ONE-TWO-THREE" rocking motion trick to get some momentum.

Skeptical but willing, they agreed to try. Lo and behold, on the count of THREE and with our mightiest push yet, the car got momentum and the driver was able to steer the now unstuck car back to the road. It was at this point when the tallest guy turned to me for a handshake and uttered those awesome three words, "You're really strong."

Now, I think we both knew I am not *that* strong. He was just trying to make sense of what had just happened, and said the first thing that came to his mind. I grin every time I think about it because what I contributed was certainly not muscle.

This girl grew up in Montana and has spent plenty of time in and around snowbanks, has helped others stuck in snowbanks, and been helped out of my own stuck situations. So I had more experience than them. Plus, with more life experience than these college kids, I knew that pushing a stuck hunk of metal uphill was nearly impossible, and with the wheels cranked so as to interrupt any momentum, we would get exactly nowhere.

Whether you're dreaming of leaving to make your own way in the world in a whole new way, or you're in the messy middle of something you deeply want to do, it's worth evaluating how much you are pushing from the front. Or whether the wheels are cranked so hard in the direction you want to go that you're not getting anywhere. It's a hard and beautiful exercise of trust to not be in such a hurry to get where you want to go that you find yourself working futilely against actual momentum.

Do What You Don't Want to Do

If you've been waiting for the arrival of motivation to start doing something about doing the boring or scary things that will expand your vistas and vision and possibilities, good news abounds: motivation, like many things in life, is *earned*.

If you've got a dream in your heart, a goal in your mind, and a longing for more freedom in your soul, stop waiting to feel like doing it. Start doing *anything* that might make it so. Stop looking for motivation to serve as your green light; rather, make your own green light by doing the small things you don't think you want to do.

Establish Where You Are

While in Lisbon, I went to the Castelo de São Jorge. What a place! After hours of wandering with a new friend—a German university student—it was time to head back to my hotel. As I headed downhill, Google Maps started acting up. By the time I reached the bottom of the hill, Maps was definitely offline. This left me lost in an area of the city that didn't feel totally safe and that was pretty fun. I couldn't navigate back to the hotel because I didn't know exactly where I was.

Figuring that out made it easy to get to the metro, and a cinch to get to the hotel.

Having trouble moving forward? Figure out where you are. Find your footing. Get firm ground under you again. Get on your own side. Identify what is actually true and what you do, in fact, know. Moving forward again becomes much more possible when you literally and figuratively know where you currently are.

There is No Timeline

We humans love a good timeline and guaranteed results within that timeframe. As it turns out, there's not much of either when it comes to building a dream.

Way more helpful is focusing on *creating* a timeline to let your dream work out as it is meant to while you keep at it.

Whose Voice is Loudest on the Airwaves?

Your thing, your way, matters. Even if it's already been done, it's never been done by you. It's also never been done the way you're trying to do it. Don't cheat yourself and us by trying to be just like everyone else.

When you are tempted to ignore your intuition or find yourself loving your thing less, take a look inside, see whose voice is getting the most airtime, and adjust the dials accordingly.

Finish Your Commitment, Then Decide

Often the right decision is to finish your commitment because you said you would. Film the course, publish the book, hold the event, deliver the goods.

And sometimes the right decision is to cut your losses, make things right with customers or vendors, and not waste more energy going down the wrong road.

You get to choose.

Dreams Require Good Infrastructure

When you see dozens of European cities in less than a year, a person starts to notice things like infrastructure. In one particular place I visited, traffic lanes seemed to be more of a suggestion for what drivers might do if they so chose. Police vehicles drove with their lights on all the time, and often their sirens as well. This did not mean they expected anyone else to get out of their way, though. If they actually wanted *that* to happen, they would get on a loudspeaker.

Potholes abounded, as did garbage in some areas. There were gaping holes in buildings, right next to fancy, new hotels. It was the sort of place where I thought twice about walking under balconies. "Crushed by a falling balcony abroad" was a travel story I didn't particularly want to collect. Alleys functioned as actual roads and during countless Bolt rides I rode with my eyes closed, sure we were going to scrape the corners of buildings. And sometimes we did. But that was not a big deal there; they would just spray paint over the scrape on their car.

People also seemed able to burn anything, anytime, and did. This made for one extremely eerie walk home from dinner as Google Maps couldn't navigate the maze of alleys. It literally abandoned me down one dark alley road and I had to navigate based on gut intuition, all while trying to ignore the thought of who might be lurking in the abandoned and derelict homes I was passing. To add to the, ah, smoky ambience, stray animals roamed freely.

Lack of critical structure makes for great travel stories, incredible pictures, and is truly one of my favorite parts of adventure traveling off the beaten track. A place with limited infrastructure has its own charm to visit, but *living* there would have its challenges.

Similarly, if we want to build something beautiful, some basic infrastructure really helps. Just as that cool city could've used a few things like fewer potholes, meaningful traffic lanes, and maybe less burning of stuff whenever you want, we dreamers are also served by basic routines of happy everyday living. You'll have your own, but consistently taking good care of the time, money, and stuff you already have is a worthwhile place to start. No figurative or literal hanging balconies 'round these parts.

Stopping to Assess Your Next Moves

You get many of your best answers on the go.

But sometimes it's worth pausing to plan your next move.

Just like a basketball player will pull up on a drive, or after receiving a pass to assess options and choose her next direction, we get to do the same thing in life. If you're feeling stuck, it might be just the right thing to do to figuratively "pull up" and start to look at what moves you might make.

New opportunities open up after you've dribbled for a few seconds. You pivot enough and all of a sudden you have better passes. New plays become options that weren't when you were originally racing down the court.

Check Who's Driving

Unhappy? Check to see if Ego took control of the wheel of the bus. Indicators that it or its cousin, Fear, has, include a dreamer hiding at home or chasing things like:

The easy road.

Acceptance from others.

Status from others.

Vanity metrics of success.

These'll distract you—all day long—from at least trying to do your thing, your way.

It's All Working Out

Find all the evidence you can that things are working out—fabulously—for you and your dream.

Evidence to the contrary is infinitely louder, and infinitely *lamer*.

So look for evidence of your progress.

Write about it.

Focus on it.

Remind yourself of it.

And celebrate every step you've taken and every "failure" closer you are to your dreams; most people wouldn't even have dared.

When in Doubt

When in doubt, make a list of what makes you and your dream wonderful, and why you are *just* the one to sponsor and bring this dream to life.

Start to like and develop your voice. Your figurative voice and also your actual voice.

Stop censoring yourself, following everyone else, or being so careful.

Start paying attention to what makes you, you, and what you like, especially as you take risks:

Cool doorways

Rock walls

How people look when they *really* smile

Birds

Humor and wit

Trees profiled against an approaching twilight sky

Mosaics

Interesting political commentary

The sparkle in some people's eyes

Construction—watching it, not driving in it

Figuring out public transportation

Sports movies

Not everyone appreciates the unique combination of things you do. Notice, appreciate, embrace your varied interests—they're what set you and your dreams apart from all the other cool people and cool dreams running amuck out there.

Explain with Caution

Avoid explaining what you're still figuring out.

Turns out our parents were on to something with their favorite answer to our incessant demands for explanation for why things were the way they were: "Because."

If you're one of those people who's always been really sure of your own mind, I extend to you a big handshake and my sincere, if jealous, congratulations. For the rest of us who have had to *work* to trust our own intuition and preferences, we know that it's easy to get swept up in explanations with anyone who asks questions about your life or your dreams.

It is a gift to take your own counsel, to trust your own mind and decisions in a settled, reasoned way. When your plans are evolving—as they are meant to, I might add—people will want to know how things are working out, what exactly you're getting up to, how it's all working out, why you left the good job, why you've made all the decisions you've made, and on and on.

You're figuring it out, it's working out, and you did it "because"—that's what. No explanations required.

Follow with Caution

It's hard to follow your way into something of your own.

Especially if you're a dreamer trying to build any kind of creative endeavor. There will be thousands of influencers ready to sell you their digital courses, their masterminds, their challenges, their coaching packages, their signature systems. Some of their advice is fabulous, but that doesn't automatically mean you should follow it. It is the easiest thing on the planet to fill your schedule consuming and implementing advice from even a single influencer without actually making headway. But most people don't just follow a single "expert"—if one is good, more is better, right? Wrong.

I heard once that the best way to deal with a charging moose is to run away, in a zig-zag pattern. My source on this shared that supposedly these lumbering herbivores can't change directions very fast and zig-zagging confuses them. An alternative approach is to do what my petite grandmother did when she was charged by a young bull moose on their country road. Grandma planted all 4'11" of herself on the gravel road, waved her hand-carved walking stick, and hollered with everything she had. At the last second, the moose decided to do something other than trample Barbara, something for which we're all grateful.

Back to the zig-zag pattern: Whether you're running from a moose or toward your dreams, it's a terrible way to make progress. I know. Bouncing between the advice of multiple experts or blindly following the advice of even a single "expert" can take you down an expensive road that wasn't even yours in the first place.

It's easy to feel like you are doing your own thing when you're actually mostly busy consuming content from someone else. It's almost like living at a motivational seminar, where the hype is super real and you feel like you're making your dreams come true. But you never actually listen to yourself, your intuition, what God's telling you, and start having ideas of your *own*.

Check Your Assumptions

While writing parts of this book, I visited family in California. After days of winter writing from a bedroom they'd generously converted into an office for me, my uncle asked if I was warm enough. People will ask the darnedest questions when you wear things like unseasonable and bulky scarves indoors. I said, "No, but I can bring the heater in. No biggie." He then asked a deeply profound question: "Is the vent open?" What a concept—vents should be *open*. Of course I knew this, I just hadn't thought to check. I'd assumed that this back wing of the house is colder because it doesn't face the sun. Wrong-o.

You might be facing a mountain, feeling like the one or two visible paths to the top are too steep or you've already tried them. But when you start actually looking, you realize you have options. There is an absolute *plethora* of side trails that switchback and wind their way up the side of the mountain to the peak.

Assuming that only the few options you can see with your blinders on are the only options in existence—EVER—is like holding shut the door to any other possibility. It often takes shockingly little constructive effort to get new ideas, rule out possibilities, or find surprisingly simple ways around what you've considered written-in-stone requirements. A journal session, a conversation with a trusted friend, asking "What haven't I considered?"

Sometimes your journaling, conversations, and research will confirm that your assumption is actually true. But, and this is a big but, I can guarantee that making even a tiny bit of effort to move your thing forward will help you realize where you're overcomplicating things. Or it will deliver some next step or new stroke of genius for making your way up that mountain of yours.

Prioritize Your Dream

Lots of things are going to be important to other people, but this doesn't necessarily make them important for you. As Greg McKeown, the author of *Essentialism* says, "If you don't prioritize your life, someone else will."

If you're going to do the brave thing or venture, you're going to start shaping your own priorities and what it is you're creating.

Beware the Cracks

So much of life disappears between the figurative sofa cush-ions of life. You know how it goes: You come back from the gym and know you need to get ready for the day, but you sit down on the bed and check your phone "really quick." Oh Nelly, that's not your best idea, even if we all do it.

Well, everyone except for the woman I read about recently who gets by with a *flip* phone and no laptop. Let me repeat that: This professional *writer* has no smart phone and she has no computer. She intentionally chooses to use a typewriter, and uses the computers at the library to do Internet things and to type up her pieces. And she's only in her thirties, so not the gray-haired grandma you might have been picturing. She's like the poster child for privacy and presence in an age where the rest of us scroll, post, and check notifications willy-nilly.

Pretty mind-bending. But I am almost positive that she has a sofa, so let's collectively get past our shock over how on earth a card-carrying member of Gen Z chooses and manages this, and get back to the sofa cushions of life we were talking about.

You pick up your phone to "check something really fast." Twenty minutes later, you're finally getting in the shower. Then, while you're getting ready, you check something else on your phone and there goes another nine minutes. And on and on. We do some version of this throughout our days and lives. You intend to do things like read more, but can "never find time." Except your phone screen time tells a different, truer story. Our screen time usually feels good and sometimes important in the moment, but how much of it advances our goals? If your usage is like mine, not much.

We're inundated with notifications, even while we work away at the stuff about which we deeply care. And even when we have notifications off, like trappers of old we might find ourselves going to check our figurative traps—email, social media, favorite apps—to see if there's anything new there. Even if you have "something in the trap," what you're looking for—meaning, fulfillment, satisfaction—will never be there.

What we're looking for is always to be found in real life. *Living* is the real deal. The most important parts of life and certainly not your dreams do not happen on a screen, even if they play an ideally-small part in facilitating them. Even our laptop-free Luddite friend in London has screens she has to interact with to keep parts of life and dreams humming along; she just is on-steroids-intentional about their role in her life.

What can lovely people like us do to keep our potential from falling into the sofa cushions of life? Here are some ideas that work for me when I implement them:

Find healthier ways than scrolling to unwind.

Use Do Not Disturb mode liberally.

Set timers for focused work.

At the end of a day, make a plan for what you plan to accomplish tomorrow. Plan B: Make one at the start of the day.

Pull the Internet tab you're actively working in into its own window.

Batch small tasks and make a game out of seeing how many you can accomplish.

To break up with the habit of immediately doing the thing that just popped into your mind and which suddenly feels very important, write it down somewhere, anywhere. If it wasn't even important enough to write down, it certainly wasn't important enough to derail your important work.

You do not have to be perpetually available to everyone who wants you to be. There is no rule that you need to respond immediately to every text or outreach you happen to see.

Given that we all have our own sofas and circumstances, you'll have your own strategies that help. It just matters that you identify your own figurative cracks and what you want to do about them. You've got interesting thoughts to think, beautiful things to create, interesting things to read, privacy to enjoy, people to help, peace to feel, and need more uninterrupted-by-tech time to do so. Heck, in your purposeful striding throughout your day and life, you might even need more *actual* sofa time—curled up watching the rain, rediscovering your love of reading, or watching foreign films.

A Letter For the Hard Days

This little letter is for the days when dreaming feels really hard. When no one else sees you or your dreams, and when they feel impossible and like yes, you really will end up working at Kentucky Fried Chicken. Nothing wrong whatsoever with good ol' KFC or anyone who works there—all work is honorable and sometimes I think I could genuinely be very happy working there.

Life can be hard for all of us. Money troubles, changing relationships, loneliness, rejection, uncertainty. We dreamers also signed up for an extra dose of hard, given the risks we are willing to take, the uncertainty we choose, the failures we're willing to make publicly, the invalidation and criticism we might get, that sort of thing.

So if you need to cry, cry. Temporarily wallow in your favorite figurative mire if you must. Vent to someone supportive. Question all your life choices. Know you have loads of company from others trying to do things they find worthwhile. Then get up tomorrow, stay in the game, and keep crawling, stumbling or marching—whatever you can muster—toward your dreams and your future. The life you're living right now, the future you're making possible, and the person you're becoming as you do are so worth the effort.

Accept Offers Carefully

Of course it's always a compliment to be recognized and to be offered bigger projects and opportunities that seem like they'll build your success castle. Maybe you'll say yes, maybe you'll say no. Just be careful about saying yes to anything solely because of money or title.

Would accepting this offer add to the fun of your life, to the growth of you as a person, to using and developing natural talents and abilities that serve you and your life as a whole? Or will it detract from you becoming who you envision or limit your personal autonomy? If so, proceed with caution.

You've got to be the one to get and stay in charge of your growth trajectory and assess even "good" opportunities for fit. Otherwise, you get sucked further away from your actual potential or hopes for your life. This may mean carefully weighing and possibly declining offers to advance or be involved in a creative collaboration that sounds amazing, but isn't in the direction you know you want to go.

Look at life through a lens of growth that matters to *you*. Sometimes, offers will come that you could not have anticipated or even known to seek out. You may choose to accept these and make a trusting pivot. But if I've said it once, I'll say it many more times: No one on Earth gets to know more than you what your dreams are or what your full participation in life looks like.

Just Say No

We've all heard it, and the lucky ones learn that it's true: "'No' is a complete sentence."

And it matters that you learn to say it. Saying no to everything that *isn't* your priority or something God has put in your heart allows you to say an enthusiastic yes to what *is* your priority.

Creative Fuel or Quicksand?

You're not here to watch other people really *live* their lives while you only exist.

Watching stuff is not inherently bad. I do it. You do it. We all do it. Well, except my grandma. She doesn't watch anything. But everyone else does, and it's not bad. But when it's numbing your ambition and your curiosity and your ability to work on projects that enhance the quality of your own life and those of others, it's not awesome.

We all do some version of this when we binge shows or spend hours of our weeks watching other people live some version—real or fake—of life on all the streaming places. We're consuming life versus creating it. It might sound like I'm judging, but I'm really not. I'm just a big fan of people living a real life that matters to them. And there are commonalities in a life that matters, and one of those is taking action. Being a creator versus a consumer.

Remember my cousin Dan the Actor? What if, instead of even *trying* to do something with his natural love of acting, he only spent his hours watching other people do the thing he dreamed of and wishing he could? That'd be sad. The irony is that, these days, he actually watches *more* media, but the motivation is entirely different. Yes, he's entertained, but he's more so studying his craft, being inspired in and by it. It's active participation, not passive or numbing consumption.

Even though writing, not acting, is my craft, I've found myself similarly intrigued by books and media that highlight writers, comeback stories, and comedians. But again, my interactions with this content are no longer driven by passive feelings of "*Gosh*, I wish I could do that." These days they're driven by curiosity and positive, creative feelings of, "I'm *doing* the thing and am here for additional creative fuel or inspiration for material."

And that makes all the difference.

Check Your Excuses

Right now might be a perfect time for a chat with your "favorite" excuses. You either get your excuses or the results you want.

Closely-clutched excuses love to hold you back from running your race.

They also specialize in keeping you mediocre and "comfortable."

Just remember, there's someone else in similar shoes to yours who's doing the thing anyway.

Consider Doing It Your Own Way

If you're not loving your results, maybe it's because you're tired of following everyone else.

Maybe try doing it your own way. It's your road after all, and in an increasingly AI-generated-content world, originality—things which could only be created by a person with your unique combination of experiences, personality traits, weaknesses, quicks—is going to matter more than ever.

Also, maybe you're more of a leader than a follower.

More of a move-making maverick than a compliant consumer.

Some of the most interesting success stories are the ones where someone decided they were just going to do it their own way. Their example gives the rest of us permission to say, "Wait, that's an *option*?"

It is.

Silence Doesn't Mean No

Word to the wise: Don't make silence in any of its forms mean more than it does. Silence just means that someone is taking time to think about something you shared or offered—your work, your idea, your words.

Catch is, there's no telling how long they will need to think about it. It may be one second, one week, one year, five years. No matter how long the silence lasts, it doesn't mean it won't work, they don't like it, or what you said was lame. Err on the side of thinking whatever is generous to you and everyone else involved.

They may be still thinking about what you said.

They may be thinking over how you can work together.

They may be having an off-day and be out of good words for responding. Or maybe what you said didn't land profoundly with them, and that's perfectly all right.

Something you shared with another person ages ago may turn into something.

You don't know, you don't have to know, and that's a relief.

Just because parts of your venturing and trying have seemingly been met by silence or no's, don't make those mean more than they do. Which is exactly nothing. Their time just hasn't come—yet.

Look At the Long Run

Throughout her book *Thinking in Bets*, Annie Duke talks about "resulting." This is a fun thing we do where we judge our decisions by the outcomes. If the outcome was good, we say the decision was good. If the result was bad, well then we hurry to say that we made a bad decision.

We hear these judgments of others all the time, and sometimes are the lucky recipients of them. We say and hear things like, "I could've told you *that*." Or, "I knew it wasn't going to work out."

Or, "She should've waited to…". Or "I knew that idea wasn't going anywhere." Really helpful stuff, isn't it?

Duke proposes an alternative method of evaluating decisions, one I much prefer because it just feels *true*. She suggests we evaluate the decision-making itself, separate from the result. To illustrate this case, she shares the example of a CEO who considered his decision to fire the company president as a "bad" one. Why? Because the results were pretty bad. Sales were falling and the replacement search wasn't going at all well. People felt lousy.

Duke helped the demoralized CEO and his leadership team review their decision process and as they did, they came to the conclusion that they'd actually made a really good decision which just happened to have bad results. It was only when they evaluated their decision in the *near-term* that they felt so crummy about themselves and their decision.

It's for this reason that I feel like we need a law which says that failure must always have quotation marks around it. Like so: "FAILURE." Let's say that in this example, the company ends up hiring a president who leads an unprecedented surge in growth and dramatically revolutionizes the company. At that point, all the decision-makers would look back on the formerly "wrong" decision to fire the lame president and simply reframe it as a hard decision that IN THE LONG RUN worked out.

As it turns out, most things work better than we could anticipate—in the long run. We do our best to make good decisions in the near-term but stop berating ourselves for the immediate results. The long run is where our biggest dreams and favorite results are made possible.

Favorite Questions to Ask

Sometimes you don't need answers or advice. You just need some different questions. Here are some of my favorites:

How can I make this fun?

How can I make this simple?

What am I actually trying to do here?

What do I want to do?

What do I not want to do?

Who needs what I'm creating?

What is my gut telling me is the next right thing?

What can I *remove* from my to-do list?

What can I do *today* to hopefully prevent the things on my worry list from happening?

If I was forced to pick just one thing to prioritize *today*, which one would I pick?

Use Your Imagination Helpfully

Here's something fun: Imagine your current hard situation as part of a feature film that will be made about you one day.

Years ago, a friend was in the thick of her medical school rotations. She shared once that on miserably cold, sleep-deprived mornings, she would pretend like her snowy drive to the hospital was a scene in a movie about her cool life. It made the miserable morning a little less miserable since she could see it as critical material for the movie of her life.

This friend made herself into the main character we all love watching triumph after pushing through months of hard days in service of her goal. Yes, it's way more fun to read about OTHER people doing hard things for their dreams, and the movie version does a lovely job polishing and neatly summarizing a long road into a two-hour movie. With stirring background music—that always helps. All the sacrifices and efforts we make don't feel very fancy or interesting or purposeful in the moments and months, unless we use our imaginations to frame things in much more colorful tones.

We can use this trick when we momentarily lapse in discipline or belief or face setbacks or feel like nothing's working out. In these moments, imagine yourself as the hero or heroine of the plot who picks themselves back up. They begin again to do things like, oh, shower. They clean their house, they take up running, they start carrying themselves erect instead of slumping through life, they start doing something (again) about their dreams, and as they rebuild, they are reborn with new humility and confidence. Gosh! I'm tearing up and have a thrill of exhilaration even just *typing* this.

This whole business of creating something of your own and using your imagination to see it that way is you writing the script for your own "success" story as it's unfolding right now. And even before it makes it to the silver screen, this can be *the* movie you play across your mind. Of all the movies in the world, the movie of your life should be, by far, the most interesting film in the world to you.

Thought Audit

Imagine your thoughts as a quantifiable commodity.

When a bank or credit card tries to be helpful and tell you how much money you've spent on various categories, they categorize them into major buckets like Food, Bills, Subscriptions.

Imagine conducting an objective thought audit, and lumping all of your "thought spending" into the following two simple buckets:

- Helpful

- Not Helpful

This framing reminds us that certain thoughts are simply not in service of what we're trying to create. They won't help us get anywhere we want to go, and they're not very fun or helpful in the here and now either.

Put another way: Is this thought going to take you up a gorgeous mountain, or plunge you into mud?

Breaking Down to Break Through

Some days you're just going to feel lost and hopeless. Even with a grounding faith, family and friends, and an abiding feeling that things *are* indeed working out, you can still feel lonely a lot of the time. Creativity can be lonely. Building something new or new-for-you can be isolating. You'll discover new depths of every emotion, and new ways in which you may feel defective. It's terrifically exciting. But even on these days you'll get up, put your pants on, get ready for the day, and do in that day what you can.

On some other days, you will feel on top of the actual WORLD. You'll feel like you'll never have to wrestle with anything ever again, like you've finally turned the corner and can see "it" all working out. It feels like every ounce of effort is paying off, the dots are connecting, and the way everything happened makes sense. We love these days.

We like the hard days much less, but just as our muscle fibers have to continually be broken and healed throughout our lives to be strong, the fibers of a soul bent on doing something worthwhile with its life and creativity have to break and repair over and over. The best news is that breakthroughs often follow the breakdowns we'd love to avoid. Knowing this sure doesn't make the latter any easier, but easier was never the point.

Proportions to Remember

Proportions to remember for building your dreams and a meaningful life of your own:

3/16 Having at least an idea of where you want to go

1/2 Taking brave + productive + consistent action

5/16 Simplifying + fixing

Be Your Best Coach

If you've never had anyone believe BIG in you and your potential, *you* get to be the one to believe in you. Even if you have a whole stable of cheerleaders, it's your turn now to believe in you—big. The God who made you certainly believes in you; you wouldn't be here otherwise.

Speak positive things to yourself. Cheerlead and celebrate your efforts and every win, even and especially the small ones.

Don't wallow. Or, wallow, then get out of the mire fast.

The best coaches never tell their players "You can't do this." Instead, they breathe confidence and encouragement into their players. Be that kind of coach for you.

Trust That the Dots Do Connect

Steve Jobs is famous for his quote that, "You can't connect the dots looking forward; you can only connect them looking backwards."

But have you read the rest of the quote?

> "So you have to trust that the dots will somehow connect in your future. You have to trust in something—your gut, your destiny, life, karma, whatever. This approach has never let me down, and it has made all the difference in my life."[17]

Only from the present can you look back and see that because you chose to do or bet on Thing A, Things B-F were made possible. And this made Thing G a possibility or helped you realize Thing H. And on and on. Eventually, all the dots do connect into a life well-attempted and well-lived.

If you don't see them connecting in this present moment, the day *is* absolutely coming when they finally do.

Let Yourself Feel Ordinary

Somewhere along the line, this dreamer picked up a belief that, if I was working on my goals and dreams, I would feel radiantly joyous and energetic every blooming day. Yes, RADIANT. While I do often feel joy in my life, I attribute this way more to my faith than I do to my pursuit of creative work that matters to me.

Some days spent building your dreams will feel totally lousy. Lots of days will feel pretty darn ordinary. *You* may feel plenty ordinary. And none of these mean a thing; a handful of elusive positive feelings have never been the goal of a meaningful life.

The goal is growth; digging deep, then deeper, then deeper—I think you get the idea—to excavate your potential. Then using that potential to create and do more than live on autopilot. On this worthwhile path, you get lower lows and higher highs than you can ever get on the status quo road of least resistance.

And even as you feel ordinary, you will also have access to a veritable library of more attainable and long-lasting feelings. Anyone interested in feeling more contentment, fulfillment, or—my favorite—the "I did it" feeling of satisfaction? I thought so.

GET THE PDF: As fun as it is to focus on dreams ahead, it's incredibly worthwhile to reflect on how far you've already come and the "trail markers" you'd share with fellow dreamers. Use the questions available on the PDF at emilyburnett .me/dreamer to get you celebrating your *own* adventures and wisdom.

5

FIELD NOTES

I n 1920, Ernest Shackleton set out with an intrepid crew to try and be the first ones to cross Antarctica by foot. They weren't the first to discover it, but Shackleton was doing the next best thing as a sanctioned expedition of the British government. Can you even imagine getting to go to Antarctica on someone else's dime? Maybe that's why people become scientists and such.

I can't bring myself to spoil the plot entirely for you, so I'll just share the following since any synopsis would give it away. Shackleton and his men never even *made* it to Antarctica, and they all survived. But boy oh boy, did they ever have the adventure of their lives. Those lives were very much a touch and go situation for just, oh, more than a YEAR. Thankfully, they had the foresight to keep journals—way to go, you guys!—making us lucky to have their well-documented highs and many more lows, at least by our standards. Their remarkably sunny attitudes throughout are an inspiration.

This final section may not be exactly diary entries. My actual life has never been on the line. I have never had to eat seal meat or survive the roughest seas on Earth. But the adventure that has been leaving safety and my life in The Wild has been my own type of adventure and one you might appreciate for yours.

This section is my chance to share a few of my stories with you to fuel your own stories and provide solidarity in your own adventuring. Many of them are about actual travel because the parallels to figurative exploration and life off the beaten path are many. And it was in traveling, literally as well as figuratively in The Land of Uncertainty, where I started to see this whole "being a dreamer" business differently.

I'm no heroic explorer about whom timeless stories will be told. But I am a kindred spirit who's left The Nest to scout out new territory, discover what meaningful lives have in common, and learn some pretty incredible lessons first-hand. I'm excited to share a handful of my stories with you, and can't wait to hear yours.

Life Was...Too Comfortable

Everything should have been great.

I owned a home which I loved.

I had great neighbors, the kind you trust with your garage code and a key to your house.

I had a comfortable job and a sweet salary.

I could afford plenty of travel, adventure gear, clothes, home decor, generous giving, and my savings was going up up up.

I was involved in the community and my church and had good relationships with friends and family.

I took pretty good care of myself in the ways experts typically recommend.

I had hobbies, enriched my mind, and tried to find ways to be thoughtful to others.

And yet.

I felt a pull to mix it all up.

To explore. To be less comfortable. To get more flexible.

To do something about my dreams.

To do something with my faith in a God who created us to *really live* while we're here and has plans for us we sometimes can't see ourselves.

Life was very good, but it hadn't worked out exactly the way I'd expected.

In many ways, though, my life was even better than I could've imagined as a kid. I would often say to myself or to friends, "If only our teenage-selves could see us right now!" This phrase would come up while eating exquisite foods, traveling cool places, going to movies and getting popcorn *and* a drink, paying our own way into really cool events, or on thrilling bike rides on cool bikes *we bought for ourselves.*

I'd far exceeded my childhood dreams of a good life which wasn't hard to do since it mostly consisted of a) being able to buy all the sugared cereal I wanted and b) being able to play outside a lot. Kid-Emily couldn't even have imagined all the fun things she'd be able to buy or do or see or experience as a grown-up. Adult-Emily could see how blessed I was. And yet...I was dang sure there were parts of me not being tapped or stretched. Life was too comfortable, too easy.

Finally, comfortable got uncomfortable enough to prompt some big moves. I was ready to risk and venture and get some figurative or literal bumps and bruises and adventure, and bet on me. And so I left. I decided to see what it would like to be the leading lady of my own, the one who takes on big adventures and leaves The Known behind to head into The Unknown, armed with the strength of my convictions, reservoirs of faith that this would all work out somehow, and whatever I could fit in my carry-on luggage.

Surprised in Rome

The day in Rome started with a triumph. I figured out the metro. And with some running to catch the right train, I was even on time to my scheduled tour of the Colosseum and Palatine Hill.

After the tour, a new friend and I explored our way to the San Pietro in Vincoli (Saint Peter in Chains) basilica and the Jewish Quarter where he knew he could get a halal meal. Over pizza and Fanta, we talked about family, faith, and careers, then went our separate ways. I wandered the city with awe and looking for pastries, then headed back toward my hotel.

Realizing I needed to make a quick stop at the pharmacy for conditioner meant I returned to my hotel from a different direction than usual. Which meant I saw a banner I would otherwise have missed advertising "Three Tenors' Concert Tonight." This concert was being held in what I'd misjudged to be a nondescript cathedral directly across the street from my hotel. Little did I know this cathedral is known for their amazing acoustics, something I personally discovered and had confirmed by a friend who knows these sorts of things.

The concert started in a mere ten minutes, so I whirled into my hotel, bought a ticket on my phone, brushed my teeth, put my hair up in a rare ponytail, and off I dashed. The musical cast consisted of just a string quartet, a pianist, and—shocker—three tenors, in tuxedos. The audience was I'd guess one hundred and twenty people, and we were collectively transported by the entire experience. For me, it felt like the whole evening had been orchestrated just for me, like *this* was why I'd come to Rome.

My own rapture, though, didn't stop me from getting a kick out of the woman next to me. She wore large, thick-rimmed glasses and an oversized fur coat, and her presence was as big as I remember her hair being. For much of the concert, she was on her knees on the prayer bench, clutching her hands together, almost sobbing during some of the numbers that had delicate tears rolling down my own cheeks.

As the concert progressed, though, I noticed her travel companion's patience wearing thin. For all I know, these women were only loosely acquainted, and her more demure companion didn't seem to appreciate the more flamboyant woman's commentary. When all three tenors appeared and started singing together, she helpfully and loudly informed her companion and everyone else: "This one they're all singing *together*."

When I was planning Europe, I did not have any part of that day on my list. I certainly didn't have "life-changing opera concert at cathedral" on the radar. And even if I had tried to make all of the parts and pieces happen, *I* couldn't have orchestrated such a perfect day and evening. Magic really does happen when we least expect it. But leaving what's comfortable, being up for adventure, and making ourselves more available for it is a good start. True in travels and true in our figurative travels through life.

Dinner with The Artist

For my first afternoon in Lisbon, I had booked a walking tour to hopefully get a crash course on the history of the place. PSA: Seven weeks of wandering through five European countries had a magic about it that would've been hard to match if it'd all been planned out. The downside: I didn't know nearly as much as I'd like to have known about the places I was visiting.

In my travels thus far I'd found that tours were a great way to learn a lot, meet people, and ease myself into a new place. This particular walking tour was packed, and there were dozens of us trotting after our tall, friendly, and very nervous guide.

For the first part of the tour, I was trying to listen to the guide. Feeling less chatty than my usual self, I wasn't very interested in chatting with a friendly solo traveler. At that point, I thought that I was on that tour to get some knowledge about Lisbon; conversation felt like a distraction from that purpose. Turns out, I was wrong. I was in Lisbon to meet Elizabeth The Artist. As the tour concluded, she told me about a fabulous restaurant and suggested we meet for a meal and fado music the next night. I had no idea what fado music was. The next day was fully planned. And I wasn't sure about packing in dinner with a chatty stranger. She, however, sold me with her enthusiasm for the restaurant and the owner, Maria, and my intuition told me it would be a worthwhile night.

Holy smokes, was it ever.

The restaurant was small, the menu was small, the owner was small, and only a small number of patrons were there that night. But the life of that night was big. Soul-expanding. Rich and flavorful, and I'm not just talking about the oven-grilled octopus of which I still dream.

Elizabeth has led one of the most interesting lives of any woman I've ever met. We talked for three hours about family and travel and femininity and politics and romance—the owner was hoping to line her up with an expat named Ben—and comparison. She was almost surprised by my realization that an artist absolutely cannot compare their work to another's because otherwise their art will never be their own. Her response to the concept of comparison was emphatic: "Never compare. Comparison hurts both people."

She didn't fit neatly in any box. She had pluck, opinions, vulnerability and strong stances you don't normally find in the same person. Elizabeth was very attentive to her feelings and trusted them to guide her. The flea market she'd gone to earlier in the day was not inspiring her, so she went elsewhere and found her energy replenished in the garden of an art gallery. According to her, a woman's superpower is her intuition and we need to honor our intuition.

A couple hours into our conversation, Maria the Owner closed the curtains of the large front window and locked the front door—I suspect so curious onlookers couldn't interrupt the concert—and announced that we would now enjoy fado music. Yes, we absolutely would. A nondescript short man and a nondescript short woman took turns singing accompanied only by two guitarists, one traditional and an impassive seventeen-year-old playing what I learned was a Portuguese guitar. The passion! The soul! The expressiveness! Not just of voice, but of body. They no longer seemed so short as they used every inch of their height to add emphasis and emotion to every bit of the song. Even though I had no clue what the lyrics meant, it was obvious they were singing about the human experience, about really living.

Throughout that evening and our conversation, it was as if something inside was practically hollering at me over the quiet murmur of Portuguese and English: "Listen up! Pay attention to what she's saying! I'm trying to show you something! You're an artist!"

Now. I now think we're all artists of some kind, and I think we are meant to develop whatever our art is throughout our lives. At that point, I very much did not consider myself anything of an artist. I once and only once drew a surprisingly passable duck on a sidewalk with chalk. At various paint nights, I was able to render something that looked vaguely like the original painting. I've never made pottery or sculpted a thing or wood-worked. But there are all kinds of mediums, with words being one of them. At that point, I'd not yet published my first book and didn't consider myself to be A WRITER. This, even though I'd written hundreds of blog posts, had a mostly-written book, and weeks of agendaless travel had inspired much scribbling about everything. I guess I had to scribble my way into being a writer and believing that I could. No matter whatever else I do, I will write—about people, about freedom, about funny things, about *life*—for the rest of my life. And I have God to thank for bringing it about through "chance meetings" with people like Elizabeth the Artist.

The People You Meet

Many of the best things of my life post-corporate were not actually orchestrated by me, and most involved other people. Talk about there being benefits of stepping off the beaten path.

Traveling the world, solo and unplanned, is a bit like living pre-Google. You hear things from and swap stories with people you meet, and you tend to believe them. They give you advice and recommendations and you do the same for them. Some you see again, some you don't, but you remember the stories and your life is more interesting for the interaction.

Some fellow traveler tells you about such-and-such a place, and you book a train ticket that very night to go visit. A business friend you only know from online invites you to her brother-in-law's home on the Chesapeake Bay and you go spend a couple days with three strangers despite being natively a little shy about things like this. A local guide says a restaurant called Pastinoure is THE place to go for kinkale, and off you go.

It's wonderful.

You exchange phone numbers, last names, room numbers, email addresses, and detailed travel plans at lightning speed, leaning on your intuition and natural rapport to guide interactions. There is an easy naturalness to interactions.

Britt was a friend I met in a several-week improv class. We'd just acted out a scene given no prompts and using only sound effects and made-up language. She did the actions and I did the sound effects. If I recall, an imaginary clothes iron and fire truck were involved. The moment it was over, we spontaneously high-fived and stood there side-by-side to receive our praise and feedback. We were as proud of ourselves as if we'd written and directed an entire play.

Attending FinCon—a conference for financial content creators—in New Orleans, I was chatting with Amy. She'd shared a really helpful comment in a class, and we arranged to meet downstairs to talk further. This led to "I need food. Do you need food? Let's go get fried chicken." We also ate the world's best biscuits.

At the laundromat in a new country, I met Isabella who'd just moved there for a new position with the United Nations. We exchanged numbers and met up for dinner that night in clean clothes—coincidentally at the very place my guide had recommended earlier. We talked about dating and dysfunctional work environments and global adventures.

Dinner with Eduardo, a friend from a walking tour of the city, led to us being on a snowy tour to Kazbegi on Monday, and Armenia on Wednesday. We teased each other about being each other's mother as we pointed out uneven steps and that the group was moving on. I served as his Georgian-English-to-American-English "translator" on our tours.

Fellow travelers—literal in this case but figurative too—empower each other to venture further than we might on our own. So when one of them says "Meteora is great," I'm like, "Wahoo! Let's go see what that place is like!"

It was actually in Meteora, Greece, where I became best friends for the day with a British neurosurgeon and a South Korean lawyer. Or so they claimed to be. While traveling, everyone could lie wildly about who they are and what they do. But most often tell the raw, honest truth. The three of us bought matching pendants so we had BFF mementos to remember each other by.

Friends I made in Rome and have stayed in touch with since share that Uzbekistan is the country they've been most captivated by, and suddenly it's shot up the list way ahead of Australia and like seventy other countries. And not because I'm a blind sheep, but because their approach to traveling and living resonates with me. After meeting them and sharing dinner at their apartment, I spent a week in Malta and recommended it to them. They went and loved it.

The shared mentality off of the beaten path is "if other curious people went there and loved it, then that's where I want to go." Thank goodness for the fellow travelers, the ones who also haven't "arrived" yet, but who are realizing right along with you that there is no "made it" point. The point of life is rather to create, to live more alive, explore widely, and make loads of friends along the way. To have more of those un-manufacturable, fleeting moments where you just pinch yourself that you get to be there. That you get to be having *this* experience with *these* people. BFF pendants optional but highly recommended.

Fear and Doing The Thing Anyway

I was housesitting for family in the California countryside, with no houses near enough to hear cries for help. Not that I'd needed anyone to hear them yet; my gift of an imagination just kept thinking of all the "what ifs" that might go wrong. Despite my paranoid efforts to keep the property and myself safe, I'd managed to leave the side door unlocked on one night, and then the *front* door unlocked the next.

Days later, I headed to bed, but not before I and my situationally-developed OCD quadruple-checked the doors. They were all locked. While I puttered and got ready for bed, I was doing a nice job not letting my imagination run away with itself as it's wont to do.

I'd just settled into bed when I heard the distinct sound of fingernails on glass. On the window of my bedroom. Relevant to this story is that there is not a tree or a bush or anything within one hundred feet of this side of the house. Literally not a rational thing could explain that sound. Terror is absolutely something that can wash over a person as it did me in that moment. But venturing out among the coyotes and the dark also induced terror, so guess what I did? I stayed exactly where I was and sent another prayer for safety toward Heaven. Since there was no one requiring my protection, I decided that if it was my time to depart this life, so be it. This may come as a disappointment, but literally nothing happened. I likely just imagined the sound, or my extra-fervent prayers for protection were heard.

Most of our fears are like that: Imagined and unfounded. But we all have them—the question is what do we do with and about them? I personally vote for putting the lie to them, choosing to trust God, and letting any sticky ones just come along for the ride.

Several months later, I was about to drive nine hours to Colorado where I planned to live for the summer. Backing out of a parking lot space into a traffic thoroughfare, I reached up for my sunglasses. When something moved mere inches from my hand, I shifted my car into park exactly where it sat and extricated myself with impressive speed. Then I stood there, considering my options for dealing with a quarter-size spider, whose unnatural tan color—matching exactly the color of my car headliner—made the whole situation even more unnerving.

By the time I could get the back of my SUV open for a towel to squish or swat it out, the spider had sprinted to the driver's side door frame. And before I could either swat or squish, the dumb thing took one last look over its shoulder at me, and darted between the dashboard and the door frame. Believe you me, I got pretty creative in the options I considered, but there was simply no way of getting at it. What I finally did was spray several puffs of dry shampoo into the crevice and closest vent, turned on the heat, and started my drive on high alert. Much like fighting claustrophobia in an MRI machine, I had to practice some good old-fashioned mind-over-matter thinking. Sometimes you just can't let yourself imagine a known spider dropping onto your foot or head while driving along at 85 miles per hour.

The alternative to moving forward toward my goal was standing in that parking lot, wishing the situation was different, and wasting time wondering what to do. Sometimes fear just has to go with you while you do the thing you have your reasons for wanting to do. There's no real alternative unless you want to live a quiet life of buried dreams.

Some of Your Best Parts Came with You

Once upon a time, there was a young woman who wanted to be able to provide better for herself. Spoiler alert: this young woman is me.

I'd been in my corporate role for a couple of years and the opportunity for income growth and challenge was, shall we say, limited. So, I decided to leave the ol' stable job that had me progressing at snail's pace, and move next door to Google in California for a twelve-week immersive web development bootcamp. Okay, it was not *exactly* next door to Google, but very close.

This bootcamp was tough, really tough. I was often there before 8:00 a.m. and stayed until 10:00 p.m. trying to understand what on earth they were saying. There was MUCH wondering on my part as to how I was going to survive this experience and how I was then going to find employment in this new line of work that was not coming at all naturally for me.

It felt a lot like stumbling through learning a foreign language and being asked to write legal arguments in that new language right out of the gate. Probably because that's basically what it was, minus the whole legal component.

For my first two months in the Bay Area, I rented an affordable room from a lovely retired couple. When I'd rented it, sight unseen, I didn't realize that the room was literally in the middle of their home. As in, there was a wall-to-wall upper window in my bedroom that looked out into the living room should I choose to open the blinds. Shockingly, I never did. Perhaps because the living room happened to be the room where the homeowners spent a lot of time. Their world might not have revolved around me, but the house did—literally—and that was awkward for someone who really values privacy.

I was still planning to make a go of life in the palpably expensive Palo Alto, but hadn't found a place yet by the time I needed to move out of the Center of the House. This led to a couple weeks of glamorous couch-surfing at the apartment of my best bootcamp friend, Toni. She had quickly become my Asian sister and was my main saving grace in this whole experience. We jump-roped in the back alley, took ping-pong breaks, and took way too many cookie runs to the neighboring Peet's Coffee for their afternoon half-price, half-pound cookies.

I did eventually find an apartment to rent for my remaining months in California. Pros: It was clean and well-maintained and the landlords were great. Cons: It cost a small fortune and the walls were so thin I found myself automatically responding with "Bless you" when the neighbor sneezed. He and his girlfriend had a sweet relationship from the many conversations I couldn't help but overhear daily.

Right out of bootcamp, I found a part-time job in San Jose for which I was grateful. Some income was better than no income, even if the work was tedious for my personality. Then I found work back in Utah where I tried to convince everyone, especially myself, that I really had promise as a full-stack web developer.

You see, my bootcamp was a full-stack experience and I went in doggedly determined to become a full-stack developer, by dang. I took it as almost an affront when anyone suggested I'd make a fabulous project or dev manager. "How *dare* you," I'd think. Please picture me, drawing myself up and responding with offense. "I *said* I was going to be a full-stack developer and even if it kills me that's what I will become."

Never you mind that it wasn't even what I deeply wanted to do. What I perpetually found infinitely more interesting was the employee experience, management, getting to the root of an issue or conflict, the business in general. Not exactly the stuff anyone needs or wants their full-stack developers to care about.

Becoming even a half-baked developer was a hard-fought road, and most days I'd question if there was *anything* I was good at. To say I had a major "Case of the Insecurities" would be putting it mildly. But it turns out that's just what happens when you ignore your native abilities and interests.

This is why I vividly remember the day I got a call from a blood donation center I'd donated with before. "We have an infant going in for heart surgery on Monday, and we're hoping you can come in and make a blood donation this weekend." When I called back, I wanted to know, "Was that just really good marketing?"

No, it was not. With surprise, the woman proceeded to tell me that I am a "baby donor." Apparently, my illustrious blood type—thanks Mom and Dad—and lack of exposure to a super common virus make my blood ideal for babies or immuno-compromised patients. How on Earth I was able to live so long without knowing how special my blood is, we'll never know.

This news came on a day when I was feeling utterly average. Actually, I was feeling below even that. It was a boon of unspeakable proportions to know that, just because of who I am, I have something to offer. Something independent of all the strengths I've tried to develop, learned to be good at, or anything I pretend to be. Of course, I'm glad for all the growth facilitated by a growth mindset, but I'm sure glad to know that I, just like you, have some dazzling qualities I just came with.

Wearing It My Way

I packed a single hat for Europe Round Two. It was a stocking cap in one of my favorite colors, and I had no idea how to wear it. News to very few: Europe in the winter is cold. I wore the hat out of pure necessity given that my main and only sometimes successful goal was "don't be cold." Since for most of my travels I felt profoundly unstylish, the hat was a perfect addition to the party—warm but not fashionable.

When I arrived in New York at the end of the boat journey, I settled in at an Airbnb before heading off to meet my dad at the La Guardia Airport. It was a cold December day and there were miles to walk before returning to Jersey. I'd decided to stop caring about the fashionability of the dang hat, trying unsuccessfully to blend in with it. Plopping it on my head in a way *I* liked, I began the two-hour public transport adventure without another thought of the hat. I'd wasted enough energy feeling dumb in it.

Nearly an hour later, a burly New Yorker and I crossed paths while we were both jaywalking, and do you want to know what he yelled out? "I like your hat!" Come again? I would've stopped in my tracks but that's generally not recommended when you are cutting through traffic. In a busy city. At rush hour. But doesn't it just feel too coincidental that he chose *that* day to compliment me on the very thing about which I'd spent the previous weeks being insecure? Turns out, *I* had to decide to either like or not care about how my hat looked on me before anyone else could.

And you'll probably understand that I'm talking about way more than a hat here. It's been the same for every one of my creative hopes and entrepreneurial dreams. It's become essential to like and have confidence in what I'm doing and to not get down on myself as I build and create. And all of that is much easier to do if I'm not obsessing over how I think I look in the figurative hat or how everyone else is figuratively wearing it. It's only when I decide, "Well, this is just how *I* choose to wear it" that I can venture forth and be about what I'm creating and what God wants for me.

"You're a Free Bird"

On an afternoon spent exploring a new city, I got to talking with a soft-spoken turtleneck-wearing new friend. At some point, I asked what he does for work in India. He reported that he's a nurse, and he loves what he does. When he asked me about my work, I gave him the CliffsNote version of what was, at that point, one year of post-corporate exploration and building.

I knew we were kindred dreamer friends when he "got" it, despite not being entrepreneurial himself. His response was simple and devoid of judgment: "Ah. You're a free bird."

Making It Discoverable

Well, what do you know. People can't want or celebrate the book you have written if it sits safely on your Google Drive.

I had a taste of taking responsibility for my own dream when I released my first book, *Dear Fellow Spender*. It'd been written and rewritten and I had grown tired of telling myself that I was going to publish my book—at some point. But as I got closer to putting it into the world, most of me wanted to quietly put it on Amazon with no fanfare, hope it got some organic attention, and call the whole thing good. That will always be a tempting option, but not a good one for us dreamers.

Thankfully, I had business friends encourage me to "make some fanfare" about it. This made for an extremely warm reception for this first-time author with a relatively small following and her book. It turns out that friends, former coworkers, and a shocking number of perfect strangers were eager to celebrate and promote the thing I'd made discoverable.

Freed From the Trappings

While in Florence, Italy, I went to see the handsome man every-one goes to see there. Yes, that one—the muscular young Biblical hero residing at the Galleria dell'Accademia.

But as cool as it was to see Michelangelo's David, I much more enjoyed the Hall of the Prisoners where Michelangelo's unfin-ished sculptures are displayed. According to the Accademia, "it is now claimed that the artist deliberately left them incomplete to represent this eternal struggle of human beings to free themselves from their material trappings."[18]

Profound.

In many ways, I feel as if I personally needed to live outside a comfortable material life for a couple years to be able to hold material things more lightly. And I attribute an increase in my intentional creativity to loosely breaking up with—at least for a season—material trappings. But there's that other belief of Michelangelo that feels relevant to what you're reading right now. As shared earlier, the sculptor believed that his job was just to free what already existed inside the marble by removing the excess. And I can attest to the fact that, when it comes to unearthing our creative potential and best work, it really is a chiseling away process.

It was years ago that I knew I wanted to write this next book, and had an idea of what it might be about. I wrote nearly 30,000 words in it—on the boat—before I had a better, but only half-baked, idea of what it was going to be. And then was nearly 40,000 words into a rewritten version before that vision had been further refined enough to write an *introduction* that represented the book I actually wanted to write. And then I basically rewrote and reorganized the entire book another time or three.

If I'd waited to get crystal clear about the statue I was trying to free from its marble trappings by having all the answers about content and structure, I would still be standing in front of a block of marble, thinking about it. Sharpening the chisel, journaling about it, talking about it. As much as it's been a struggle to get this book in your hands, I like to think that what the process did for me and what the book ends up doing for you was buried under every single word I wrote—the ones I kept and the very many that were edited out.

Haul Less Stuff, See More Things

Halfway through a two-week stint in Athens, I made plans to see an island. It being February, it was not exactly prime season for an island excursion. But you never know when you'll be back in Greece, and I wanted to at least see a Greek island. Given my other plans and some volunteer commitments, I only had two days and a night for an island adventure, and that seemed better than nothing.

Some islands were too far away, and many were not consistently accessible this time of year by boat, or the ferries to them could be really rough. So I settled on a close island, Aegina, and booked a night's stay at one of very few open hotels. Not wanting to lug even a carry-on size suitcase with me, I asked the hostel if I could leave luggage behind. They should've declined considering that I had just checked out, but they were happy to help. That generosity allowed me to traipse off with just my purse and my Cotopaxi bag, stuffed with the things I'd most need in case my other stuff ended up stolen from where they casually stashed it.

As hoped, traveling light made the whole island adventure infinitely easier. Navigating the trains and congested sidewalks and the port and the ferry and the walk to the hotel office and the unexpected ride on the back of a moped with the hotel owner to the unexpected satellite hotel location would've been technically possible, but tricky.

The longer I'm at this whole life business, I'm convinced that an easy life is not the goal; a meaningful one is. And being able to navigate and create and explore that life is made infinitely easier by being less encumbered—by stuff, bad habits and vices, dysfunction, self-centeredness. An easy trip to a Greek island is one thing. Doing good for others and responding to God's inspiration is infinitely more rewarding. And we can be infinitely more flexible for those pursuits and content in more circumstances if we're not figuratively lugging around one of the ginormous suitcases of an Instagram influencer in Europe for a photo shoot.

The Existential Crisis of New

It can be a totally unmooring experience arriving in a new country. "New" doesn't even begin to describe the party. "Disorienting" and "absolutely unfamiliar" were closer to describing what I experienced— it was a complicated fusion of excitement, overwhelm, and sometimes weird apathy. While I'm talking about travel, it can also apply to entering any kind of new-to-you territory, and certainly building your dreams.

Because traveling and not having a home base *was* my life for two years, I didn't have a comfortable, normal life to return to. This heightened feelings of homelessness and disconnection, but on the flip side, caused me to feel at home in a kazillion places around Europe and the United States. Once the first shocks wore off, that is.

The first day I arrived in Tbilisi, Georgia, I especially felt this way. By that point in 2023, I'd packed up forty-nine different times for trips ranging from one night to several weeks. I arrived in this fascinating country groggy, running on fumes, and not feeling very adventurous. My hotel room was clean, but all the conveniences and comforts a person gets used to in the United States—things like cozy lamps, heat, and water as hot as you like it—were in short supply. Also, you know you're sleeping on a hard mattress when you add a thin towel under the sheet for "extra padding."

As panic rose, I countered it by marshaling my courage to be brave in yet another new environment. Because, what was the alternative?

I made a list of things to do that day so as to not spend it in the world's most uncomfortable bed watching Netflix. Or worse—staring at the textured wallpaper wallowing in an existential crisis. If I really needed to, I could return to my humble hotel room and watch a show or the wallpaper, but not until I got moving and did some stuff, however small.

The small list I made for myself for the day was a bit like the "baby steps" Dr. Leo Marvin gives Bob for overcoming his crippling anxiety in the movie *What About Bob?*

1. Shower. Check. No matter how un-hot it is, a shower always makes a person feel better.

2. Connect to WiFi. Check. Small accomplishments go a long way.

3. Leave the hotel. With no pressure to go far or to see anything in particular.

4. Find an ATM. Then wonder as it whirs for an unnatural length of time what you'll do if it doesn't actually dispense your cash.

5. Find food. This one will drive even a person in an existential crisis out the door. Instead of eating cookies and soda from the tiniest corner market you've ever seen, I decided I might as well see some of the city by walking to a well-reviewed restaurant near the river.

Once out of the hotel and fortified by food, I ended up wandering more of the city to discover an art market *under* what was called in English "Dry Bridge." There I wrote and people-watched and soaked up the cold fall sunshine. Then I poked around the flea market happening *on* Dry Bridge marveling at things like the passports and military ID cards of Soviet soldiers from the time that Georgia was part of the USSR. I sure hope my personal documents are never hawked in a market.

When I asked my Instagram followers earlier in the year why they travel, a favorite answer came from a friend: "Because it's hard. It stretches me." Prior to my departure on what turned into these two years of traveling and working on my business and writing dreams and goals, I'd only heard one person, in a book, refer to travel being hard. Which either means that this particular author and my friend and I are the only three people on the planet for whom travel can be hard or who get stretched doing it. Or that others just don't talk about it.

My conclusion? The lucky ones are the ones who know we're here on Earth to be stretched, who put themselves in new territory—literally or figuratively—and who find simple ways to get their bearings in new situations quickly. The alternative is to hunker down in the hotel room, play it safe, and miss out on the whole experience you're here to have.

I'll Do It My Own Way

I was participating in a well-known marketing guru's program and officially drinking the Kool-Aid—blue flavor. A best business friend had also joined the expensive program, and we were all in on this being THE THING to grow both of our businesses. With all the hype, it almost felt like the guru was doing *us* the favor by allowing us and hundreds of others to buy her program. Funny how that works.

True to my early love-of-school roots, I was a very diligent "student" in this program. I printed out the curriculum, listened to all the morning mindset calls, attended every live call, and followed the influencer's steps to a T. Part of her method involved sending lots—and I do mean lots—of emails to our lists and posting a lot on social media. Obediently, most of us did what she encouraged. I even created a few Instagram Reels involving trending audio and some happy finger dancing. I shudder at the memory.

Now, there was nothing unethical about her recommendations even if they were rather aggressive and the promises of success were oversold. It turns out that her style of business isn't *my* style of business at all. And given what this guru shares on social media, I'm not so sure she's happy with the business she's built either. But neither she nor her course was really the problem here. The problem with at least my participation in all of it was that there was way too much lame *following* going on.

Contrast this with a guest presenter ironically and loosely affiliated with her program who casually shared that he didn't do obsessive email campaigns and he "just didn't do social media."

Come again, CJ? That's an option? In a sea of experts hollering the same advice—"Be on social!" "Slide into the DMs!"
"Send all the email!" "Follow the trends!"—CJ was like,
"Naw, thanks. I'll do it my own way." Thank goodness for
fellow dreamers like him who remind us that, when it comes
to creating something of our own, our preferences and the
recommendations of our intuition trump the recommendations of even the most convincing expert.

Ditched in the Desert

Many months ago, I was driving from Salt Lake City to San
Diego County, a drive I've done countless times. Including
the February trip when seeing what looked like the Northern
Lights coincided with Christmas music inexplicably playing
on the radio in the middle of nowhere, Nevada. I digress.

On this particular drive, I had Google navigation pulled up
on my phone. Why, I don't know since the directions for
hundreds of miles were to "drive south on I-15." A few hours
into the drive, the app made a helpful in-flight announce-
ment: "There is a 34-minute slowdown ahead." It then offered to serve up an alternative route. Great, Google—let's
do it.

Off went I and scores of others, following the alternative navigation with what turned out to be reckless abandon. A state
highway became less of a highway and more of a road. Then that
road became a crummy road. But there were still plenty of us

redirected drivers, and it seemed like things could come right in the end.

I won't bore you with all the details, but let's just say that the pavement eventually disappeared, and the rural properties became visibly less and less friendly with more "No Trespassing" signs than seemed strictly necessary in the middle of nowhere. Our cohesive string of cars turned into multiple strings of cars taking their chances on various sandy roads. So much for solidarity, you guys.

My only company on this adventure was the *Dateline* podcast about a guy who'd killed each of his wives and—get this—gotten away with their murders for *years*. Not the sort of soundtrack I'd recommend for getting lost in a foreboding desert. I hit rock bottom when I found myself, alone, parked in front of a sign about the size of a medium pizza box. It said verbatim: "No I-15 Access. Extremely Rough Road. No Cell Service. No Services. AWD High Clearance ONLY." Behind the sign, the sky was tar-black and as menacing as you've ever seen a sky. I'm no survival expert, but I know that flash floods in the desert are no laughing matter.

There were no other cars to follow at this point, and my super helpful navigation guide kept urging me forward on the Road of Despair. I made a thirteen-point turnaround on the washed-out sandy road, made a series of turns that felt promising, and eventually got myself out of the pickle Google had put me in.

When it comes to waking up and taking chances for your dreams, there comes a time when you've got to figure certain things out for yourself and trust your experiences. You've got to figure out what *you* actually want, what really matters, and whether you're creating your own dream or someone else's. And just as I learned on that day in the desert, sometimes you've got to go against what the experts say and blaze your own path forward. It's your life after all.

Creating Through Resistance

In the book, *The War of Art*, Steven Pressfield talks about what he calls Resistance. This is the super fun force that doesn't want any one of us to create, and a force we've got to expose as a big ol' liar every day by taking meaningful action to make our things possible. See the frequent visits from Resistance as evidence that you're on the right track. It has no need to visit those who are permanently camped out in the Land o' Stuck.

This Resistance likes to tell action-oriented dreamers very fun things like, "Your work is not good enough, original enough, profound enough, personal enough." When that line of accusation doesn't work on me, it may tell me that my work is *too* conversational and too personal." How something can be too personal and yet not personal enough we don't know—Resistance doesn't specialize in logic. This enemy of joy simply delights in any tactic which will squash any creative impulses.

Knowing this, I keep creating. I keep writing and dreaming and making stuff and putting it into the world. Why? Because even when Resistance is loud, I know deep down that I like writing, making, and sharing stuff, and that it's the only way of creating things that last. And even when I don't like the process or the timeline, I remember that many a creator has had to expend a lot of creative effort over time to get to the really good stuff.

So I plow on, no matter what Resistance advises. What does it know anyway?

"I Am My Best Investment Right Now"

Several months ago I decided it was the day to do one of the things I'd put off for months. Because I didn't know if it would take eight minutes or eighty minutes of my time, it was easier to put it off for eight months.

Plain and simple, I needed to transfer money from one brokerage to my IRAs at another. Not exactly rocket science, but easy to put off. One simple phone call got the task in motion, and it went from hairy and scary—okay, not scary, but unknown, and the alliteration was too good to pass up—to "all right let's just take care of this thing." Never underestimate what a woman can do when fueled by a French sandwich and looking forward to the reward of a macaron.

One phone call turned into five, at the two separate financial institutions. Three of the people I talked to were men named Nick. Does that not seem statistically improbable? It would seem like if you want your son to be financially really responsible and help others with their investments, I might suggest you name him Nick.

One of the last calls involved doing some device verification, so I pulled over and parked in front of a residence with a charming yard. As I talked with Nick on the phone, I logged into my account on my laptop perched on the center console. When the owner of the charming yard wandered out—I suspect to see what I was up to—I like to think she thought I was doing some investigative work.

Anyway, Nick wanted to run through the questions they run all customers through who've just transferred assets. He wanted to know *all* about my plans for saving and investing and retirement. This even though I told him I was in a business building chapter and was not making the same income I had been. After, like, seventeen questions, I said, "Okay, Nick, here's the deal. I totally understand your recommendations, and will get there again. Right now, though, is not that chapter for me. I am betting on *me* as my retirement plan, and doing what I need to do right now to create my own income opportunities so that I can blow your estimates out of the water."

He got it. In that moment of bold self-assertion, he seemed to believe it as much as I believed myself. Fiscally sound behaviors taught by Nicks are always a good idea. Yes. *And* we will always be our own most important investments in making our beautiful futures possible.

At Least I'll Go Out Like An Adventurer

Many moons ago, my dad asked if I'd like to go on a canoe trip with our family friend, Joe, and his adult daughter. The prospect of three days on a gorgeous Montana river with no cell service and great company made it an easy yes.

Fast forward some weeks, and we were embarking on the last day of our trip. I stood watching the raging river gush past, legitimately terrified of what was ahead. This was the day with all the hairy parts of the river: Rollercoaster Rapids, Rock Garden, and what I called the Hairpin Bend of Death. The already high river was swollen from heavy rain the previous twenty-four hours. News from the ranger that a rafter had died on this stretch of the river a few weeks prior, and certainly prior to all the recent rainfall, made my fear not unfounded.

In a private several minutes by the river, loading the canoe, I considered my options.

1. *Walk* the twelve miles alongside the river.

2. Request a ridiculously expensive helicopter ride.

3. Get in the canoe and deal with the day.

Realizing my only viable option was to *move*, I tamed my panic into a corner of my soul and finished the day's preparations. Joe and Jocelyn took off first, all 6'7" of Joe standing up in the canoe to assess the river conditions. I was still wearing my brave face when Dad remarked, "In all my years, I've never seen Joe put on a life jacket." My barely-mastered panic was back on, big time. But moments later, in strength that welled up from somewhere inside, I had the emboldening thought: "Well, If I'm going to die today, I'm going to die like an adventurer."

Spoiler alert: I didn't die. In fact, we had a great day and even laughed our way through paddling for our lives. It may not be every day that I'm literally paddling for my life, but that attitude of adventure serves me on even the days of figuratively paddling for the life of my dreams. That Helen Keller was on to something, when she said: "Life is either a daring adventure or nothing."[19]

"I Can't Wait to See What Happens Next"

A birthday reflection from the middle of my "midlife gap years."

Well, happy birthday to me! I haven't made my millions yet. This book is shapeshifting as I investigate and write about what I really think about "dreaming big" for people of faith and principles. I wonder what it will settle into. At this moment, I'm on a boat in the middle of the Atlantic, somewhere between the Azores and Bermuda. The sun is shining brightly and the only thing interrupting miles of gentle waves is the shadow of a few clouds on the otherwise shimmering surface. I sit at a table in the La Cucina restaurant wearing a tacky polyester vest I bought from a French boutique in the Azores—and sunglasses. The sun is bright—literally and figuratively.

The horizon is visible, then not visible, then visible again as the ginormous ship bobs its way over the swells. How much is that like life? We get glimpses of what lies ahead for us and have days where it seems like we'll never lose sight of the horizon. And then we do. But not for good.

Waking up, taking chances, and creating things of our own ends up being quite the dance between what we know, what we don't, and finding treasures along the way. But here's what I do know about my life, and yours:

There will be plenty of dips and downs, but there will also be many, many ups. There is always someone to ask for help. There will always be friends to make. There is always something to be grateful for. You can figure out anything you need to. It's all working out in God's time better than you can even imagine.

And I can't wait to see what happens next. The best part of any story, and what keeps you turning the pages, is that you can't anticipate exactly what's coming next.

I Wouldn't Trade It for Anything

Fourteen months after leaving corporate, I found myself on a day trip into Armenia. That was one of life's really good days. It was my first by-foot border crossing which was very exciting. As was potentially having my phone taken for taking a picture of it. Changing something like twenty Georgian lari into thousands of Armenian drams made me feel positively rich, but also, it can't be great living with that kind of currency inflation.

In a small village, we ate one of the best lunches of my life with a local family. The hero of the meal was a carrot salad. I kid you not. We visited churches and monasteries from as far back as the 5th century and I wish I would've counted the number of Lada 06 Soviet-era cars present on the roads.

We had memorable conversations on religion and regional politics with our tour guide, Luka. It was fortunate I had not managed a trip to Azerbaijan like I'd hoped to prior to this Armenia trip. While en route, Luka asked our group of five if any of us had Azerbaijani stamps in our passports. "No? Oh good." Turns out we would have—best case—been denied entrance or—worst case—detained. Wouldn't that have made for a good story? Apparently, at customs control they're not just flipping through looking for a blank page. They very much care about where else you've been.

Our small group of two Spaniards, two Chinese, and one American (me) were chatting in front of a tiny market in Odzun while we waited to get underway again. A couple had just been married in the historic village church, and the wedding entourage was moving down the rough street. They were accompanied by groups of laughing school-age children stretching string across the road and not letting cars pass until they donated money. It seemed innocent, but the reaction of one guy driving an out-of-place BMW sedan made me wonder if it was actually extortion. One of our friends from China had just been approached by local teenagers, asking if she was a famous K-Pop singer none of us knew. They were disappointed when she told them she wasn't. We laughed about this.

Even though the day was freezing cold, the sun was shining and the camaraderie between our small band of new friends could not have been better. I was soaking up this wonderful feeling of, what was it? Oh yes, just being *alive*. All that year, no matter where I was—often not in exotic locations—I'd felt more alive than I had in years. My clothes had never been less fancy or more frequently worn, and I was often the miserable trifecta: tired, cold, and hungry. But sometimes you've got to get uncomfortable to start to slay some of your dragons.

I was being changed by the people I was meeting, what I was reading in place of all that self-help stuff I used to read, and the lessons I was learning from life and God and slower time in nature and whatever place I was in. I had a mostly dependable Google Maps and a completely dependable God.

Exactly what I did may not be doable for everybody. It might not be for everybody. Heck, a lot of the time I wasn't even sure it was for *me*—not just the full-time travel piece, but the leaving everything familiar, having very little comfort zone, navigating uncertainty, learning to believe even more. To say I've been stretched more than I ever had before wouldn't begin to cover my time in The Unknown, The Wilderness, The Messy Middle.

All I know is that I wouldn't trade the experiences I've had for anything. Uncertainty makes a person start holding more lightly to material possessions and the need to understand. I found myself asking better questions and preparing for better answers.

There is a clearing of the soul when you stop trying to control and plan everything and let life do some washing over you. Rather like it very much did on that day in Armenia, and on so many other days of noticing life more, waking up to it, trusting God more completely, and taking chances to create a life of my own.

CONCLUSION

When I left perceived safety for my travels of unknown duration, I had a long list of negative what-if's rattling around in my brain:

What if I need things that suddenly feel essential for life, like pen refills and sticky notes and chapstick and American chocolate?

What if there's a natural disaster while I'm traveling?

What if my cell phone international data plan doesn't work out?

What if I don't like solo foreign traveling?

What if I can't figure out transportation options, can't get around, and end up in countries I didn't intend?

What if I get pickpocketed or, worse, mugged?

What if I can't ever get warm? Will my small wardrobe be sufficient?

What if I get sick?

What if I meet no one to pal around with?

This list went on and on.

It makes me wish I would've spent more time on *positive* what-if's:

What if it works out even better than I imagine?

What if it's even more fun than I think?

What if it's even cooler than I anticipated to be in these beautiful places?

What if I make loads of friends along the way?

What if I actually love navigating public transit?

What if, even on the hard days, I feel more *alive*?

What if I learn really cool things about myself?

What if I'm unwittingly planting things that will yield unanticipated fruit when the time is right?

Boy, if this isn't like a giant analogy for a life with big dreams. There are so many negative (or what we see as negative at the time) possibilities, and creating things of our own sure *can* involve a lot of hard and cold and lonely. But also, it can be GRAND.

I hope you know and remember more than ever, that your dreams matter. A lot. That your dreams are guaranteed to change, that you will grow into dreams you didn't even dare or know to dream.

That you're not a malcontent if you don't like your job or want to change in your business or creative endeavor or want to move across the country "just because." There's a ginormous difference between being a constant complainer and knowing that you want something more for yourself, that you don't just want to take what opportunities have come to you, but that you want to see about creating your own opportunities.

That you stop chasing other people's dreams or even worse, their faux dreams—of prestige, of fancy cars, of the biggest houses.

That you stop waiting for things to get safer or more certain before you act on ideas God may actually want you to act on.

That you start using your agency to create an even more wonderful life for yourself, those you love, and whoever God wants you to help with it.

If I do my job, a year after you read this book, your own book may be well underway.

You may have finally left the job in which you were absolutely shriveling for a job that interests you, even if you had to take a pay cut to do so. Or you might've started or ramped up your side hustle and be getting closer by the day to leaving your job to take a chance on it. Maybe you'll have decided to stay where you are, but to change how you show up in it: solidly taking the reins of your life and increasing your personal autonomy.

You may not only have started voice lessons but have joined a choir. You may have landed your first acting gig, opened the coffee stop for which your community is practically begging, traveled to Antarctica to see the seas that Earnest Shackleton and his team of intrepid explorers survived against all odds, found an art mentor and submitted your first painting to the state fair. Maybe you'll have discovered how meaningful it feels to coach Little League or volunteer weekly or start going to church again.

And none of this because you've got a life you're trying to escape, or because you're trying to earn anything you can't, like worth. But because you, Fellow Dreamer, are—exactly as you already are—worthy of doing something about your dreams and listening to the longings of your soul.

Ready to get to it, for the first time or for the umpteenth? I thought so. We dreamers have got more of that most rare of all pursuits—living—to be about.

Endnotes

1. Ralph Waldo Emerson, "Self-Reliance," in *Emerson's Prose and Poetry* (2001), 121.

2. "Vincent's Life 1853-1890: Looking for a Direction," Van Gogh Museum, https://www.vangoghmuseum.nl/en/art-and -stories/vincents-life-1853-1890/looking-for-a-direction.

3. David Epstein, *Range* (2019), 125.

4. Carl Richards, email to subscribers, February 22, 2024, refer-encing https://behaviorgap.com/radio/the-personal-thing-seri es/.

5. "Samuel L. Jackson Biography," IMDb, https://www.imdb. com/name/nm0000168/bio/.

6. "Laura Ingalls Wilder," Historic Missourians, https://histor icmissourians.shsmo.org/wilder-laura-ingalls/.

7. Wayne W. LaMorte, "Behavioral Change Theories," Boston University School of Public Health, https://sphweb.bumc . bu.edu/otlt/mph-modules/sb/behavioralchangetheories/beh avioralchangetheories6.html.

8. "Stages of Change Model," Loma Linda University School of Medicine, https://medicine.llu.edu/academics/resources /stages-change-model.

9. Brad Klontz, Rick Kahler, and Ted Klontz, *Facilitating Financial Health*, 2nd ed. (2016), 51.

10. Jerry Seinfeld, commencement address at Duke University, May 2024.

11. Ralph Waldo Emerson, "Self-Reliance," 132.

12. "Jimmy Stewart Suffered Extreme PTSD," Daily Mail, https://www.dailymail.co.uk/news/article-3825552/Jimmy -Stewart-suffered-extreme-PTSD-lost-130-men-fighter-pilot -WW-II-acted-anguish-filming-s-Wonderful-Life.html; "Jimmy Stewart's War Service," VZCM, https://www.vzcm.org/featured/blog-post-title-one-cxfyw.

13. "Seven Things You Might Not Know About 'It's a Wonderful Life,'" National Endowment for the Arts, https://www.arts.gov/stories/blog/2022/seven-things -you-might-not-know-about-its-wonderful-life.

14. Philip Van Doren Stern, *The Greatest Gift: A Christmas Tale*, https://www.amazon.com/Greatest-Gift-Christ mas-Tale/dp/1476778868.

15. Timothy Ferriss, *The 4-Hour Workweek* (2007), 44-45.

16. LinkedIn post, June 26, 2025, https://www.linkedin.co m/feed/update/urn:li:activity:7344014946109669376/.

17. "'You've Got to Find What You Love,' Jobs Says," Stanford News, https://news.stanford.edu/stories/2005/06/youve-got-find-love-jobs-says.

18. "Michelangelo's Prisoners/Slaves," Accademia Gallery, https://www.accademia.org/explore-museum/artworks/michelangelos-prisoners-slaves/.

19. Helen Keller, *Let Us Have Faith* (1940).

EMILY BURNETT is no stranger to risking for her dreams.

She left a comfy tech career of nearly ten years in 2022 to spend time exploring her way around Europe and the U.S. while pursuing her own dreams. Since then, she's learned that a meaningful life rarely follows a straight line and that some dreams can only be discovered by taking chances.

Rooted in faith, freedom, and fun, Emily likes talking with strangers wherever she travels and considers herself at home in the western United States.

Hey, fellow dreamer!

If this book resonated with you, I'd be grateful if you'd leave a review on Amazon (scan below) or Goodreads. Your honest thoughts help others like us find this book, and grows the movement of principled dreamers taking chances, staying in the game, and creating lives of their *own*.

For additional writings, find me on Substack at More to Your Life (moretoyour.life). This is where I share sometimes funny stories, travel mishaps, and personal essays about what makes life cool and people interesting.

Also, I love hearing from readers. Feel free to drop me a line at emilyburnett.me/books.

It is infinitely easier to take action on your dreams when your financial roots are healthy and organized. If you are interested specifically in the overlap between money and making your dreams possible, you may enjoy *Dear Fellow Spender: Enjoy Using Your Money to Get Out of Debt, Build Savings, and Create a Life You Love.*

In this book, I write about how I finally came to trust myself with money, navigated my own debt-payoff journey, and how others can do the same. I write in relatable, hopeful ways about the art and pleasure of taking care of your money to create the life you want.

Available now at emilyburnett.me/books.